C000196383

THE RIBBLE WAY

About the Authors

Both natives of Lancashire and living not far from Preston, Dennis and Jan Kelsall are no strangers to the Ribble Way and the splendid countryside through which it runs. As professional outdoor writers and photographers, they have written and illustrated many guides covering some of the country's most popular walking areas. They also contribute to various magazines, and for many years produced a weekly walking feature for the *Lancashire Evening Post*.

Their enjoyment of the countryside extends far beyond a love of fresh air and open spaces and an appreciation of scenery. They also have a keen interest in the environment and its geology, flora and wildlife, as well as a passion for delving into the local history that so often provides a clue to interpreting the landscape.

Other Cicerone guides by the same authors
The Pembrokeshire Coastal Path
Walking in Pembrokeshire
The Yorkshire Dales: South and West
The Yorkshire Dales: North and East

THE RIBBLE WAY

by

Dennis and Jan Kelsall

2 POLICE SQUARE, MILNTHORPE, CUMBRIA LA7 7PY
www.cicerone.co.uk

© Dennis and Jan Kelsall 2005
First edition 2005
ISBN-10: 1 85284 456 6
ISBN-13: 978 1 85284 456 1
Reprinted 2010 (with updates)

Printed by KHL Printing, Singapore
A catalogue record for this book is available from the British Library
Photos by Dennis Kelsall

OS Ordnance Survey® This product includes mapping data licensed from Ordnance Survey® with the permission of the Controller of Her Majesty's Stationery Office. © Crown copyright 2009. All rights reserved. Licence number PU100012932.

Acknowledgements

Dennis and Jan Kelsall greatly appreciate the help and information they were given by rights of way staff at Lancashire and Yorkshire county councils and the Yorkshire Dales National Park while they were researching this guide. Thanks are also due to the staff of the Lancashire and Blackpool Tourist Board, and the Preston, Ribble Valley, Settle and Horton in Ribblesdale tourist information offices. Many other people have also contributed in a host of different ways, offering advice, information and hospitality in true northern fashion. To them all, the authors wish to extend a very warm thank you.

Advice to Readers

Readers are advised that, while every effort is made by our authors to ensure the accuracy of guidebooks as they go to print, changes can occur during the lifetime of an edition. Please check Updates on this book's page on the Cicerone website (www.cicerone.co.uk) before planning your trip. We would also advise that you check information about such things as transport, accommodation and shops locally. Even rights of way can be altered over time. We are always grateful for information about any discrepancies between a guidebook and the facts on the ground, sent by email to info@cicerone.co.uk or by post to Cicerone, 2 Police Square, Milnthorpe LA7 7PY, United Kingdom.

Front cover: Heading north beside the Ribble from Clitheroe

CONTENTS

The Ribble Way

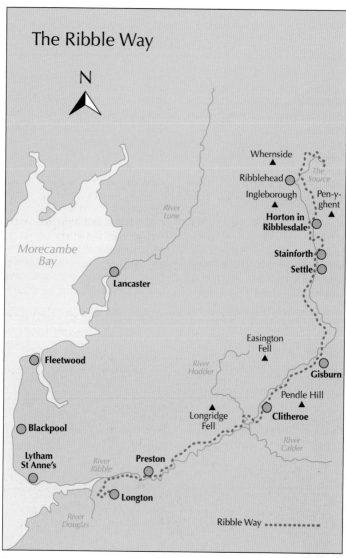

N

Whernside ▲

Ribblehead ○

The Source

Ingleborough ▲

Pen-y-ghent ▲

Horton in Ribblesdale ○

River Lune

Stainforth ○

Settle ○

Morecambe Bay

Lancaster ○

Easington Fell ▲

River Hodder

Gisburn ○

Fleetwood ○

Pendle Hill ▲

Longridge Fell ▲

Clitheroe ○

Blackpool ○

River Calder

Lytham St Anne's ○

River Ribble

Preston ○

Longton ○

River Douglas

Ribble Way ● ● ● ● ● ●

INTRODUCTION

Although Lancastrians might like to claim it as their own, the River Ribble actually springs from limestone high on Cam Fell in the heart of Three Peaks country, in the Yorkshire Dales. Gathering water from the countless streams that spill from this sombre upland, the river quickly asserts its identity as it forces a passage between high, rugged moorland hills. Eventually breaking free to meander through gentler countryside south of Settle, it still has another 10 miles (16.1km) to go before broaching the boundary with Lancashire. And Yorkshire folk with long memories will remember an older border between the rival counties that ran south of Sawley, and they might say that the river remains in Yorkshire for a further 10 miles (16.1km).

By then the river has assumed a completely different character, winding lazily through alternating pasture and ancient woodland, where old manor houses and early-18th-century cottages offer a welcome contrast to the all-too-pervasive tide of modernity. At Preston the river encounters the only sizeable conurbation along its course, but even here it remains largely

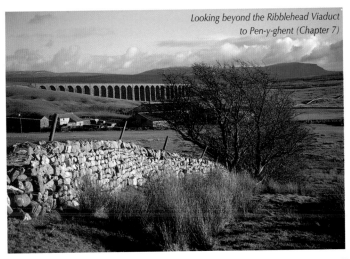

Looking beyond the Ribblehead Viaduct to Pen-y-ghent (Chapter 7)

*The River Ribble beside the
De Tabley Arms, Ribchester (Chapter 3)*

isolated from the commerce and industry of the city. It flows instead below the elegant Victorian parks that were laid out for the recreation of the thousands of workers brought in to operate some of the first factory mills built in the country, replacing what had previously been a cottage industry.

Beyond Preston the river changes dramatically yet again, now running straight to the Irish Sea through an almost featureless plain that was once regularly inundated by the tide. Dykes and drainage ditches have turned what was once a virtually dead-flat waste into productive arable fields, although further to the west a vast expanse of the salt marsh still remains, attracting huge populations of birds, particularly in winter, which find a rich and plentiful source of food in the shallows and mud.

THE RIBBLE WAY

The idea for a long-distance footpath along the course of the River Ribble originated in the 1960s with the members of the Preston and Fylde group of the Ramblers' Association. The original survey suggested a mainly riverbank route from the mouth of the Ribble, where it flows into the Irish Sea, to its source far above Gearstones, a former drovers' inn beside the moorland between Ribblehead and Widdale. This plan immediately ran into difficulty, however, as more than half the proposed way relied on the use of private fishermen's paths. Further progress was thwarted by a storm of local objection, and it was not until the 1980s that an alternative route adopting existing rights of way attracted official support. The first leg of the

The start of the Ribble Way at the edge of the salt marsh (Chapter 1)

The final leg across Gayle Moor above Gearstones (Chapter 7)

path, covering just over 40 miles (almost 65km) between Longton and Gisburn Bridge, was opened by Mike Harding, president of the Ramblers' Association, and Derek Barber, chairman of the Countryside Commission, on 1 June 1985.

Because the Ribble Way follows the south bank of the river, a coastal start to the walk was, and still is, frustrated by the lack of a convenient crossing over the River Douglas, which joins the Ribble on the same bank around 3 miles (4.8km) from the sea. The lowest bridging point across the Douglas is that spanned by the A59 some 5 miles (8km) above the confluence of the Douglas and the Ribble, so if the walk started from the coast, this would involve a good 10 mile (16km) detour up to the bridge and back to the confluence again.

But as soon as the Ribble Way opened, it was extended in the other direction, beyond Gisburn Bridge, right to the source of the river. (The route was devised by the late Gladys Sellers, author of the first Cicerone guide to the Ribble Way.) Since then there have been several marked improvements to the way, including, for example, a new section of path at Hurst Green which skirts the woods above the river and avoids the need to climb onto a road. More recently a path opened through Gisburne Park, which in bypassing Gisburn eliminates a long and disagreeable walk along the busy A682. On the downside, however, one of the most picturesque sections of the route was lost to the public in 1999 when a landowner successfully contested the legitimacy of the riverside right of way between Sawley and Gisburn.

You will always find ducks beside the river at Sawley (Chapter 4)

*The riverbank at Cuerdale,
just outside Preston (Chapter 2)*

The 70½ mile (113km) route that has evolved does not always run right beside the river, as was first envisaged. Nevertheless, it remains within the broad confines of the valley, and proponents of the original scheme might concede that an advantage of this occasionally elevated course is the expansive views it offers over the surrounding countryside.

The Ribble Way moves from one side of the valley to the other, generally making use of road bridges to cross the river. However, at Hacking Hall, where the River Calder joins the Ribble, there used to be a ferry; but with the death of the ferryman in 1954, it ceased to operate. Although it would seem there had always been an intention to replace the ferry with a footbridge, by the time the path

was opened the bridge was no nearer to reality, though many hoped that the establishment of the Ribble Way and the resulting increase in use of the riverside footpaths would help to revitalise the scheme. However, conflicting opinions as to whether the Ribble Way should be routed over the Ribble, the Calder, or the Hodder further upstream, not to mention a lack of financial resources, left the project on hold. The new century brought a ray of hope when an innovative design was unveiled for a bridge linking the separate paths at the confluence of the Calder and Ribble. Had the plan come to fruition, the need to detour via Lower Hodder Bridge would have been removed, and many new possibilities for local walks would have been created. Unfortunately, the economic climate changed and the plan was abandoned, but who knows? Perhaps one day…

There is still hope, too, that the landowners at Sawley may have a change of heart and once more admit walkers to a splendid section of the river. No doubt other changes will occur over the course of time, for like the river itself, nothing is constant.

LANDSCAPE

Despite the river's relatively short length (75 miles/171km), it travels through a great diversity of landscape. The bleakness of the slate, grit and limestone hills that surround its source at Ribblehead is in sharp contrast to the richly green alluvial plains that fringe the watercourse amid the rounded slopes of central Lancashire, and the vast reclaimed marsh through which the river escapes to the sea gives no hint of the lush, wooded banks to be found further upstream. Although for much of its way the river squirms vigorously within the confines of a broad valley, its general course is relatively uncomplicated. After initially aligning almost with the meridian to break from the hills at Settle, later it is gently turned onto a westerly trend, in search of the open sea, by the outliers of the Pennine Moors. But today's river is a mere shadow of the mighty torrent of meltwater that originally gouged out the valley. This meltwater was released as vast ice sheets began to retreat in the face of a warming climate, barely 12,000 years ago.

On the slopes of Park Fell climbing Ingleborough (Chapter 7)

Approaching Ribchester (Chapter 2)

INDUSTRY

In contrast to many of the fast-flowing rivers that originate in the Lancashire and Yorkshire Pennines, the Ribble is hardly touched by the industry and conurbation of recent times. The only towns of any size on its banks, Clitheroe and Settle, appear to turn their backs on the river, and even the flourishing city of Preston largely ignores its presence. Things could have been very different, though, for in earlier times the Ribble was both a source of power and a means of transport.

The great abbeys of Fountains and Furness held extensive tracts of land in upper Ribblesdale, and throughout the medieval period wool production, as well as some mining in the surrounding hills, were important industries. Downstream the land came

within the influence of the abbeys at Cockersands, Whalley and Hornby, and while sheep again prevailed on the higher ground, cattle, oats and hemp were farmed within the valley. By the 16th century an important linen industry had evolved, later switching to cotton as trade with the New World developed. Fulling and dyeing were cottage industries, carried out in small mills on farms and in villages by rivers, until the mechanisation of the weaving and spinning processes brought the advent of the factory system at the end of the 18th century. The water power of the river fuelled the developing factory system, and the construction of the Lancaster and the Leeds and Liverpool canals helped establish Preston, and even Settle, as industrial centres. Had the Leeds and Liverpool Canal been looped around

Balderstone and Whalley, as initially suggested, it would no doubt have spawned a succession of factory towns along the Ribble east of Preston, but in the end the canal followed the Calder valley and Blackburn and Burnley grew as industrial sprawls instead.

The crucial moment of change occurred with the invention of the steam engine. This immediately demonstrated its superiority over the mill wheel and, even better, was not dependent upon the vagaries of the weather. Industry quickly regrouped around the coalfields, and along the canals and expanding railway network, where coal could be delivered relatively cheaply. Many of the early factory sites that were not so well placed gradually faded into obscurity, and consequently, unlike the neighbouring Colne and Calder valleys, that of the Ribble has remained largely rural – not a bad thing at all, and may it always remain so.

WILDLIFE

But although the Ribble valley has remained rural, this does not mean it is a botanical paradise, for intensive agriculture and grazing have marginalised many wildflower species and the insects and other types of life they support. However, numerous stretches in the middle sections of the river are rich in natural woodland, with a few areas demonstrating continuity with the original 'wildwood'. Here, particularly in spring, a variety of native tree and shrub species, such as oak, ash, alder, beech and hawthorn, shelter an abundance

Geese on the Ribble near Alston College (Chapter 2)

Riverside meadows can become almost park-like in summer (Chapter 5)

of flowers, while hedgerows and the limestone uplands also support a range of flora. Bluebells, ransoms and primroses are common, while violets, orchids, speedwell, cowslips and campions are among the many others you will spot.

Birds are a constant companion along the length of the path, from those congregating around the coast, to the hill and moorland species that inhabit the higher regions. In winter the marshes attract massive flocks of geese, while gulls are prolific throughout the year. Herons, guillemots, coots, moorhens and, of course, the ubiquitous duck are plentiful. Oystercatchers are common, and lapwing, curlew, plover and snipe haunt the higher reaches. Kingfishers are to be seen along the riverbanks, and in the woods and hedgerows you will find songbirds, many of which are familiar from our gardens. Fox and roe deer roam freely, although they are not always easy to see, for if they sense you first they will disappear quickly into the undergrowth. Should you be about during the late evening, there is also the chance of seeing a badger.

The Ribble is very much a fisherman's river, noted for its salmon, which in autumn can present a fine spectacle in the shallower sections as they make their way upriver to spawn. Other species are common, too, such as trout and lamprey, and just about every type of coarse fish is present.

PRACTICALITIES

At just over 70 miles (113km) the Ribble Way is one of the country's shorter 'long-distance' walks, and thus an ideal choice for newcomers to long-distance walking. It runs through countryside for virtually its entire length, but the path is rarely far from 'civilisation', and only in its higher reaches does it pass through a wild landscape. For the most part it is gently pastoral, although this does not mean that the challenge it offers should be underestimated. Countryside walking can be as physically demanding as hillwalking, particularly after heavy rain or during the summer at the climax of vegetation growth. Substantial boots, waterproofs, appropriate clothing and a comfortable pack are necessities, and gaiters are indispensable on wet days. Shorts are rarely a good idea unless you have hardy legs, and in summer remember to take suncream and a hat. Some route sections offer only limited opportunities for refreshment during the course of the day, unless you make a diversion, so food and drink should be carried, and it is also a good idea to have a small extra 'emergency ration' in case of an unexpected delay.

For convenience the route is presented here in seven legs, but the time taken to complete the walk from end to end will depend on personal choice and ability. No stretch of the Ribble Way is overly demanding, and most reasonably fit people should

Whernside, one of Yorkshire's Three Peaks (Chapter 7)

not experience any difficulty in completing a section. However, if you are unused to walking any distance on a daily basis, it is sensible to do some training beforehand.

Accommodation is reasonably scattered along the route, enabling a range of possible itineraries. The accommodation listing in the

Appendix is neither exhaustive nor does it imply recommendation, but is provided to assist in planning daily stages for a linear walk. Bear in mind that at weekends, some establishments may not take bookings for a single night, but staying the extra day opens an opportunity to explore the surrounding countryside. Most places can offer an evening meal, or are close to a pub or restaurant, and may be able to provide a lunch pack if you ask in advance. There are four convenient camp sites along the way, but recent years have seen the opening of a small number of bunk houses. Further information is available at local tourist information centres, details of which are also included in Appendix 2.

When to walk the Ribble Way is also a matter of personal choice. Spring and autumn are perhaps the best times of year to enjoy the colours of the landscape, while a good summer can be idyllic. Winters are generally mild, although the higher reaches of the walk are subject to the extremes of British hill weather, and excessive rainfall can be a problem at any time of year. Very heavy downfalls or prolonged wet periods will raise the water level of the river, sometimes to the extent that the path in some of the middle sections becomes impassably flooded.

When planning any long walk it is a good idea to build in some flexibility, and as the countryside surrounding the Ribble Way offers many possibilities for exploration, you will have little difficulty in finding something satisfying to occupy a spare day. The way is also very well suited to day walking, as it enjoys good public transport connections and many sections offer a wide choice of other paths from which to create a range of circular walks. Suggestions for day walkers, highlighting available transport and possible return routes, are given at the end of each chapter, and 'end to enders' might find this information useful in allowing them to extend their stay to see some of the countryside beyond the way. Longridge Fell, Pendle Hill, Pen-y-ghent, Ingleborough and

Leaving Horton in Ribblesdale, the Ribble Way passes the Crown (Chapter 7)

The path from Horton in Ribblesdale onto Ingleborough (Chapter 7)

Whernside are obvious attractions, all readily accessible from the route, while any number of uncrowded paths range across the lesser hills.

The Ribble valley is easy to reach from the national road and rail networks, with both the M6 motorway and the West Coast main line passing through Preston. A good rail service from Ribblehead simplifies getting home again at the end of the journey.

MAPPING

Route finding is not a significant problem and, particularly in Lancashire, you will have little difficulty in spotting the distinctive blue RW icon waymarks periodically used to sign the path. Elsewhere the general yellow footpath arrows and occasional informal markers identify paths, and you will need to refer to the text or a map to keep yourself on the correct route. The OS map extracts accompanying the text show the corridor containing the Ribble Way, but do not give the detail found on the 1:25,000 scale Explorer maps – for example, the path in relation to field boundaries. Day walkers and those wanting to appreciate the wider countryside through which they are travelling will find the large-scale mapping invaluable. The four relevant sheets are given below.

ORDNANCE SURVEY MAPS

Explorer 286, Blackpool & Preston
Explorer 287, West Pennine Moors
Explorer OL41, Forest of Bowland and Ribblesdale
Explorer OL2, Yorkshire Dales (Southern & Western areas)

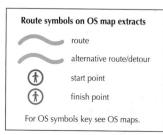

Route symbols on OS map extracts

〰	route
〰	alternative route/detour
🚶	start point
🚶	finish point

For OS symbols key see OS maps.

CHAPTER 1

Longton to
Penwortham Bridge

Distance	7.5 miles (12.1km) from the Golden Ball in Longton village, 6 miles (9.6km) from the Dolphin Inn at the official start of the Ribble Way
Height gain	125 feet (38m)
Route assessment	Quiet lanes, tracks and generally good field paths; no noticeable ascent
Time	3 hours
Public transport	Regular bus services between Longton and Penwortham Bridge
Parking	By the Dolphin Inn at Longton, and at the entrance to Priory Park beside Penwortham Bridge; also pay-and-display parking in Preston
Refreshments	The Dolphin Inn at the start of the Ribble Way and a choice of pubs in Longton and near Penwortham Bridge
Toilets	Brickcroft Nature Reserve on Liverpool Road, Longton
Map	OS Explorer 286, Blackpool & Preston

Beginning along the edge of the marsh overlooking the confluence of the River Ribble and the River Douglas, the walk later turns beside the Ribble to follow it in an almost dead-straight line towards Preston. Much of the surrounding land has been reclaimed from the estuary and is consequently rather flat and featureless, but as you progress upriver the buildings of Preston and its near neighbour, Penwortham, become more prominent, each occupying higher ground on opposite sides of the valley. Behind them, to the southeast, Winter Hill is conspicuous, the television and communication masts dotted around its summit an unmistakable landmark. Depending on the state of the tide and amount of recent rainfall, the river may present itself as anything from a disappointingly gentle flow between wide muddy banks, to a full-bodied surge lunging angrily at the flood defences. Yet whatever your first impression, you can be sure that the river will adopt many more moods during its journey. Here you see only its final stage, in which its very direct route to the sea follows a course that is at least partly the result of man's intervention. But while only occasionally dramatic, this stretch of the Ribble is not without interest – there is birdlife aplenty, and many reminders of the time when Preston was as much a seaport as Liverpool.

The official beginning of the Ribble Way is at the Dolphin Inn, otherwise known as the Flying Fish, which lies some 1½ miles (2.4km) west of Longton. However, as public transport takes you no nearer than the Golden Ball pub in the village of Longton, without a car you must begin the walk from there. Follow Marsh Lane, which leaves the main thoroughfare, Liverpool Road, beside the pub. It is a pleasant start to the walk and you soon leave the houses behind as the lane meanders across a deadflat hedged landscape. Keep going past the end of Grange Lane, but

where the main lane then bends left, carry on ahead, still on Marsh Lane, to the Dolphin Inn. The way continues beyond along a short track leading to the outer flood defence, a high grassy embankment that separates the reclaimed farmland from the salt marsh. Climb onto the top and follow it away to the right.

THE SALT MARSH

Although richly green and a good 5 miles (8km) from the open sea, the expanse below the outer face of the dyke is still liable to inundation. Even at ordinary high tide this grassy waste is broken by silvery pools and winding runnels as the rising water invades every vulnerable depression – it is certainly no place for the inexperienced to venture alone. However, the salt marsh is a rich feeding ground

Joining the River Ribble on Hutton Marsh

for birds, and in winter particularly you will see huge flocks of geese, ducks, gulls and waders. Less appealing is the flotsam washed in on spring tides and by winter storms and left stranded as a snaking line of detritus at the limit of the flood. But look above it and you will see in the middle distance a glinting ribbon that is the River Douglas.

The River Douglas has its source on the western flanks of Winter Hill and is the final tributary of the Ribble before it meets the open sea some 3 miles (4.8km) to the west.

This is the obstacle that prevents the Ribble Way from beginning at the coast, as the nearest crossing over the Douglas is the A59 bridge south of Tarleton, which would necessitate a lengthy and uninspiring detour from the course of the Ribble. ◀

During the early days of the Industrial Revolution the River Douglas was made navigable as far upriver as Wigan, so that coal could be transported to the sea for export around the coast and to Ireland.

After ½ mile (800m), swing right with the dyke as it drops alongside Longton Brook to a field access and live-stock pens. Instead of simply crossing the culvert, the Ribble Way traces a circuitous route around the enclosures. Over consecutive stiles just to the right, briefly follow the hedge left to another stile. Tackling more stiles, cross a track and then the brook itself. Some 30 yards to the right along the opposite bank, a final stile leads into the corner of a large field. Following the fence away from the brook, maintain your direction as you later cross a farm track and another field, eventually regaining the embankment. The River

Ribble soon appears ahead, the levee turning upstream beside it to take the Ribble Way on towards Preston.

MANAGING THE RIBBLE FOR LAND RECLAMATION AND SHIPPING

If allowed to follow its own inclinations, the river would dissipate across a broad tidal estuary. The almost geometrical embankments that now contain it served the two-fold purpose of reclaiming fertile land and rendering the river navigable for maritime trade. However, the wash of the tide from the sea and the silt brought down by the river are liable to obstruct the channel, and during the heyday of shipping regular dredging was necessary to maintain sufficient draught for sea-going vessels.

Posts embedded at regular intervals along the riverbank were used to anchor the dredgers, and some still trail mooring cables and chains into the silted banks below.

THE LANCASTER CANAL

A little further upstream on the opposite bank is the outflow of Savick Brook, recently made passable to allow pleasure barges access to the Ribble from the Lancaster Canal. Begun in 1792, the canal had originally been intended to run between Wigan and Kendal via Preston and Lancaster. ▶

The plan involved taking the waterway across two major rivers, and although an aqueduct was built spanning the Lune upstream from Lancaster, there was insufficient capital to finance the considerably greater engineering feat of crossing the Ribble valley. As an interim measure the canal company filled the gap between the truncated ends with a tramway to convey cargoes, but the additional costs and delays associated with double-goods-handling meant that the canal failed to achieve its potential, and then the railway age arrived before it could be completed.

The Lancaster Canal was constructed to transport coal, textiles, gunpowder and other manufactured commodities as factory production became established in Lancashire.

The revival of canals as a leisure resource during the latter half of the 20th century reawakened interest in joining the two halves of the Lancaster Canal, and in 1981 the Lancaster Canal Boat Club put forward a scheme to connect the northern part of the canal to the River Ribble along the course of Savick Brook. As Savick Brook is lower than the canal, locks were needed to enter this section of the waterway, with another lock downstream to retain water at low tide, and it was 20 years before the work was finally completed. Now boats can pass into the Ribble from above Preston, go on up the River Douglas to Tarleton, and join the main Leeds and Liverpool Canal system along the Rufford Branch.

PRESTON'S SKYLINE

Even at this distance Preston's buildings command the horizon. Gone are the tall chimneys of the mills and engineering factories on which the prosperity of the city once relied, and in their place rise the tower blocks of commercial enterprise and housing. Another relative newcomer breaking the skyline is the latticework stadium of Preston's football team, North End. ◀

Preston North End was a founder member of the Football League and is one of the few clubs in the country still playing on its original ground.

It houses the National Football Museum, and even if you are not particularly a fan you will almost certainly find the displays and exhibitions fascinating – you can even try your hand as a 'guest commentator'.

Some outlines that would have been familiar to travellers passing this way a century ago remain, however, perhaps the most prominent being the white spire of St Walburghe's Catholic Church.

St Walburghe's spire was designed by John Hansom, the same man who gave us the Hansom cab. Soaring to 309 feet (94m), it is the third highest in the country and was built by the Jesuits between 1850 and 1854. Although the church is of dun-coloured sandstone, the towering landmark spire stands separate from the church and is of a contrasting white limestone that shines in the sun. It is said that much

The eye-catching spire of St Walburghe's Church

of the stone for its construction was bought second-hand from the railway companies as they replaced the stone sleepers supporting the track with wood.

Shortly after passing the outlet of Savick Brook on the opposite bank, the raised grazing narrows and the route progresses over stiles across a culvert carrying Mill Brook. Now left to its own devices the bank assumes an unkempt appearance, going first beneath successive power lines carried high above the river on massive gantries, and then past the entrance to Preston Docks on the far bank. After skirting a golf course continue at the fringe of Priory Park to walk beneath the A59 bypass. This is now the lowest crossing of the Ribble, an honour formerly held by Penwortham Bridge a little further upstream.

PRESTON DOCKS

The docks were opened in 1892 and at the time boasted the largest dock basin in Europe. They served a town rapidly developing on the back of textile manufacture and quickly became some of the busiest in the country. Warehouses, oil tanks and loading cranes once formed a backdrop to the ocean-going cargo vessels that came and went on the high tides. Preston remained a working port into the early 1980s, but despite the advantage of its proximity to both the rail and motorway networks, the dockyard's reliance on river access rendered it inaccessible to larger vessels, and trade consolidated on the better-placed docks further south at Seaforth and Bootle. The basin has, however, found a new lease of life, and since the area's redevelopment for housing, retail and leisure, is once more as busy as it ever was. ◀

Preston Docks were named after Prince Albert Edward, Victoria's eldest son, who finally succeeded his mother to the throne at the age of 60, only nine years before his own death.

PENWORTHAM

The historic old town of Penwortham sits on top of a prominent hill rising above the Ribble's southern bank. It developed around a motte and bailey castle that overlooked an ancient fording place there. The Romans appreciated the strategic importance of the site and were the first to establish a fort here, a commanding position that remained in use throughout the Saxon period, and after the Conquest the Normans, too, established a base. ◀

In 1075 Benedictine monks from Evesham Abbey founded a priory, and it was probably they who first began draining the surrounding marshes to create new farmland. The priory has long since disappeared, and all that remains of the castle is the artificial earth mound.

Penwortham was one of the few places in Lancashire to be mentioned in the Domesday Book at a time when the area was largely considered an unproductive wasteland.

The oldest building still standing in Penwortham is the 15th-century church dedicated to St Anne, whose squat square tower can be seen through the trees upon the hill. Tradition holds that there has been a church on the site since 644 AD, a not improbable claim given the sustained significance of Penwortham during those early times, when travel across the sea to Celtic Ireland would have been a less daunting prospect than an overland journey to York or Canterbury. As with many churches in the country, St Anne's was heavily restored by the Victorians – a practice intended as a proclamation of the prosperity that the industrial age had brought. ▶

Beyond Priory Park a track takes you beside allotments to meet the main road at Penwortham New Bridge, over which the Ribble Way crosses to the river's northern bank.

PENWORTHAM OLD BRIDGE

In the middle of the 18th century a bridge was built at Penwortham to replace the ford and ferry which had until then been the only means of crossing the river this far downstream. The bridge collapsed after only four years but was succeeded in 1759 by a more substantial structure. That survived until 1912, when the present bridge was constructed to meet the demands of a new vehicle on the roads – the motor car.

One of the entrepreneurs who helped create the wealth of the industrial age is buried in a railinged tomb in St Anne's churchyard. Born outside Bolton in 1768, John Horrocks opened Preston's first factory cotton mill and went on to establish a textile business that became one of the largest in the world.

DAY WALKERS

Unless you retrace your steps along the Ribble Way, it is a 4 mile (6.4km) walk back to Longton, mainly along busy main roads. The most sensible alternative, therefore, is to take a bus, and while it will be easier to find convenient parking in Longton, leaving a car in Penwortham or Preston in the morning and catching a bus to Longton avoids having to wait for one at the end of the walk. The choice is yours.

CHAPTER 2

Penwortham Bridge to Ribchester

Distance	11.9 miles (19.2km)
Height gain	830 feet (253m)
Route assessment	Quiet roads and lanes; riverside and field paths may be muddy after rain; beyond Preston the countryside is undulating with some short but steep climbs and descents
Time	5¼ hours
Public transport	A bus service between Preston and Clitheroe stops at Ribchester
Parking	Car parks in Ribchester and Preston (pay-and-display)
Refreshments	A variety of pubs and cafés in Preston, with three riverside pubs between Penwortham and Walton Bridges; then there is nothing along the route until you reach Ribchester, where the village offers a choice of pubs and a café
Toilets	At Preston bus station and beside the car park in Ribchester
Maps	OS Explorer 286, Blackpool & Preston, and OS Explorer 287, West Pennine Moors

The route around Preston is a surprising haven of calm compared to the frenetic activity of the nearby city centre. It follows quiet streets and passes through pleasant parks along the banks of the river, and also heralds a change in the character of the Ribble valley, for it marks the point at which the river breaks free from the surrounding hills. Upstream, the watercourse snakes within a wide plain, batted from one side to the other by steep bluffs of dun-coloured sandstone. The formal geometry of the efficient drainage system, outlined by ditches, that could be seen in the field patterns of the estuary is replaced by more natural boundaries that follow the lie of the land. Ragged copses of gnarled woodland and stretches of old lane and hedged track give the countryside a more ancient appearance. The hand of man is in evidence in old manors and farmstead buildings, some of which date from the 15th century. More distant views hint at the wilder landscape to be encountered later in the walk, while closer to hand there is great variety in the plants and woodland trees lining the way.

Despite the construction of the A59 bypass road, Penwortham New Bridge remains busy and is best crossed on its northern side at the traffic lights. The onward way hugs the riverbank along Broadgate, Riverside and then successively at the edge of a sports field, Miller Park and Avenham Park. Beyond that is a playing field, after which The Boulevard takes you past the outflow of the River Darwen, on the river's opposite bank, to another of Preston's main arteries, the A6 road at Walton Bridge.

PRESTON

Historically, Preston was the lowest point at which the Ribble could be bridged, and certainly it has no shortage of crossing points today. Upriver of Penwortham New Bridge is the graceful five-arched Penwortham Old Bridge, still standing but closed to traffic, while just beyond it stand the gaunt piers festooned with a jumble of service pipes and cables that once carried the West Lancashire Railway from Southport. Further on, the high and much-widened bridge overshadowing the Continental pub carries the West Coast main railway line into Preston Station, which lies just a few hundred yards up the hill to the north. The next bridge also served a railway, this time from Blackburn and the east, but trains are now routed round by the main line and the bridge is left for pedestrians, as is the next one at the far side of Avenham Park. In a way this last bridge is the most interesting, for it was built to carry the tramway that connected the two halves

Penwortham Old Bridge

of the Lancaster Canal, and which ran from a basin in Aqueduct Street, northwest of the city centre, to Johnson's Hillock beyond Whittle-le-Woods, a distance of some 8 miles (12.9km). The trucks were horse-drawn for most of its length, but stationary steam engines were

employed at either side of the river to haul and lower trucks along straight inclines to the bridge. The present metal structure

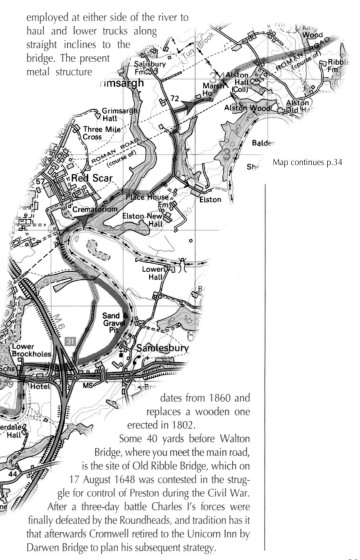

Map continues p.34

dates from 1860 and replaces a wooden one erected in 1802.

Some 40 yards before Walton Bridge, where you meet the main road, is the site of Old Ribble Bridge, which on 17 August 1648 was contested in the struggle for control of Preston during the Civil War. After a three-day battle Charles I's forces were finally defeated by the Roundheads, and tradition has it that afterwards Cromwell retired to the Unicorn Inn by Darwen Bridge to plan his subsequent strategy.

Preston claims Saxon foundation in the seventh century, and with charters later granted under Henry I and Henry II, was undoubtedly a medieval town of some importance. It sent a representative to Parliament from as early as 1295, but sadly no buildings from those early beginnings have survived. ◄

The only memorial to Preston's several ancient gates is in street names such as Fishergate, Friargate, Bishopgate and Stoneygate.

In his *Tour of the Whole Island of Great Britain* (1724–6) Daniel Defoe remarked that it 'has a great many gentlemen', but it was the industrialisation of the later 18th century that moulded the town we see today. Richard Arkwright invented his water frame for spinning cotton in Stoneygate, paving the way for a textile industry that helped Britain dominate world trade throughout the Victorian era.

Despite the considerable redevelopment of recent decades, Preston retains many of the fine Georgian and Victorian buildings that arose as a result of the burgeoning prosperity brought about by the factory system. Imposing crescents of terraced mansions and gardened squares overlook the river, while around the market square are civic buildings as fine as any in the country.

Many of Preston's greatest buildings are due to the generosity of a single man, Edmund R Harris, who bequeathed his family wealth for the provision of a public library, museum, orphanage, institute and schools.

If you have not already begun the day in the city, the best way to visit from the Ribble Way is to follow the path up from the head of the old tramway bridge.

Preston's several parks date from the Victorian period. ▶

Moor Park at the northern end of the city was one of the first public parks in the country, and was laid out on common land that had been granted from the Royal Forest of Fulwood by Henry III in 1235. Those by the riverside are fine examples of Victorian Romantic landscaping, and form natural amphitheatres overlooking formal walks and gardens by the water's edge. Avenham Park was the setting for the first Mormon baptisms conducted in Britain, which took place on 30 July 1837, establishing a link that is perpetuated today in the splendid Mormon temple built on the outskirts of nearby Chorley, and dedicated in June 1998. The imposing brick building above Miller Park was built as the Railway Hotel, and once provided a meal for Queen Victoria as she passed through Lancashire on her way to holiday at Balmoral. The queen ate 'take away' style in the privacy and luxury of her own railway carriage, while the more adventurous Prince Albert apparently took his refreshment in the station buffet.

The parks were places of recreation for both the wealthy and the ordinary folk, whose dreary factory labour maintained the entrepreneurs and gentry in their comfortable state.

Miller Park and former Railway Hotel

During the second half of the 20th century Preston's traditional industries of cotton and heavy engineering began to decline, and for a time, at least, economic prosperity was uncertain. More lately, however, an influx of commerce and diverse light industries has heralded a revival, and there has been a rapid expansion of housing and other new buildings. Already famous for its Guild celebrations, held every 20 years (hence the saying 'once every Preston Guild'), recently Preston has firmly established itself as the cultural and economic focus of central Lancashire. ◄

In 2002, on the occasion of the Queen's golden jubilee, the town of Preston was awarded city status – the Jubilee City – and the parish church of St John the Evangelist was elevated to a minster.

Over the dual carriageway, follow a track past a parking area to a fork, where a stile on the right returns you to the riverbank. Progressing upstream past the tidal limit a new face of the Ribble valley is revealed, a wide, flat-bottomed alluvial plain bordered by scarps and hills on either side, drawing your gaze towards the as yet distant bulk of Pendle Hill. Eventually joining a track from a farm, Mete House, continue along a riverside promenade at the edge of Melling's Wood. The profuse spread of trees and plants is an appetiser for things to come, with beech, birch, ash and other trees shading a flowery carpet that in spring bursts with colour. Beyond the wood, the path skirts a golf course and ultimately leads out to another main road, the A59.

BURIED TREASURE

On the opposite bank, where the river sweeps in curves across an old flood plain below the road and motorway bridges, workmen digging drains in 1840 found a cache of silver treasure buried in the silt of the riverbank. It contained around 10,000 Scandinavian coins as well as a number of ingots, all stamped with dates before 928. It is unlikely that a single individual could have amassed such wealth, and it is thought that the hoard belonged to an army, and was perhaps lost in an attempt to ford the river.

Pass beneath the flood arch and join a concrete track towards Lower Brockholes Farm. Approaching farm buildings, turn off right on a broad, enclosed path between the fields, closing with the river to pass beneath the motorway and slip road bridges. The continuing drive ahead leads to the car park and visitor centre of Brockholes Wetland Nature Reserve, created from the flooded depressions of old quarries that exploited sand and gravel, washed from melting glaciers at the end of the last ice age. However, the Ribble Way offers a choice of routes. You can remain with the riverbank along a permissive path that leaves over a stile to the right of the reserve entrance, or alternatively you can follow Ribble Way signs left beside the motorway slip road and then swing right along a causeway between the extensive lakes, semi-natural woodlands and unimproved grasslands of the reserve, eventually emerging at the far side into open pasture. Here the two paths re-join and you should bear left to the top corner of the field, where a ladder stile leads into Boilton Wood.

Flooded gravel pits at Brockhole Quarry

Crossing Tun Brook

To the left a path climbs away through the trees and shortly meets open ground. Follow the perimeter around to the right, slipping back into the woodland fringe at the far end above Red Scar, a high bluff of sandstone that turns the river in an abrupt bend below. Later emerging into fields, bear right and remain parallel to the trees over successive stiles. In the fourth enclosure veer right to find a stile into Tun Brook Wood, from which a path falls steeply to a footbridge at the bottom. After climbing to emerge in fields once more, strike out to a gate in the far-right corner, there joining Elston Lane.

TUN BROOK WOOD

For the next few miles the river runs within a relatively wide and straight valley, although its course is deflected from side to side by the abruptly rising scarps on either side. Where the ground is too steep for cultivation, either overlooking the river or beside the stream gullies that drop from the surrounding hills, copses remain from the ancient woodland that invaded the valley after the last ice age. None is more extensive than Tun Brook Wood, which cloaks a deep side-ravine for over 1½ miles (2.4km). Native species such as oak, ash, hazel, alder and holly have been allowed to regenerate naturally over the centuries, and the damp, fertile soil nurtures a splendid assortment of wildflowers, with snowdrops, ransoms, bluebells, arum, wood anemones and orchids among those most easily identified, each in their appropriate season.

Follow Elston Lane away to the left, going left again when you reach a junction. After some ¾ mile (1.2km), and approaching the high point of the rise, look for a waymarked farm track leaving through a gate on the right. Stay ahead past the buildings of Marsh House farm, continuing through a gate along a hedged green track. Around a bend at its end go over a stone stile adjacent to a gate on the right and walk away beside the left-hand hedge. Carry on in the next field, passing

The River Ribble below Tun Brook Wood

a pond and aiming for a house that becomes visible at the far side. Leave over a stile behind the house and walk out to Alston Lane. Regaining the fields over another stile directly opposite, keep walking forward, later descending to cross a brook running at the base of a shady dell. Maintain your direction across subsequent fields and ditches, passing left of an oak in the third pasture to drop beside a hedge into another wooded gully. Climb away beyond, following the edge of successive fields and eventually joining a track beside a cottage. Follow it out to Hothersall Lane.

DARWEN TOWER

The previous couple of miles have roughly followed the line of a Roman road, and the elevated, open aspect gives a splendid panorama across the broad valley. In the distance to the southeast are the Pennine moors, distinguished by Darwen Tower and the forest of transmitter masts adorning Winter Hill. Darwen Tower was built to commemorate Queen Victoria's diamond jubilee in 1897, but more poignantly symbolises the success of local people in winning free access onto the surrounding moors in the previous year.

Follow the lane to the right as it drops back into the valley, curving at the bottom past the Hothersall Lodge Field Studies Centre. As the lane ends, keep going forward past Hothersall Hall, passing through a couple of gates to climb away along a fenced track. Where that bends, cross a ladder stile on the right and make for the top of a wooded bank above the river. Skirting the trees, Ribchester comes into view beyond the crest, the way falling to a gate near the bottom right-hand field corner. Progress from field to field, eventually joining a hedged

The river from above Hothersall Hall

The riverbank at Ribchester is a popular picnic spot

track that cuts off a bold sweep of the river to reach a farm, and then continues past St Wilfrid's Church and the Roman museum to a junction at the lower end of the village. The centre of the village and its amenities lie up the street to the left, while the onward route rejoins the riverbank beside the primary school opposite.

DAY WALKERS

If you follow the Ribble Way just a little further on to Ribchester Bridge, there is a meandering return on the opposite bank. This adopts lanes and field paths through Osbaldeston, Balderstone and Samlesbury, and thence continues largely beside the river into Preston. However, this would create an unreasonably long walk of some 25½ miles (41km). A much better strategy if arriving by car is to park in the morning at Ribchester and catch the bus to Preston. From the bus station it is then a 1 mile (1.6km) walk past the museum, market square and along Fishergate to the beginning of this section at Penwortham Bridge.

CHAPTER 3

Ribchester to Brungerley Bridge

Distance	11.5 miles (18.5km), or 10 miles (16km) once Hacking Ferry Bridge is in place, possibly in 2006
Height gain	874 feet (266m)
Route assessment	Undulating field paths and tracks, with short sections along lanes
Time	5¼ hours
Public transport	Bus services to Ribchester from both Preston and Clitheroe
Parking	Car parks at Ribchester and Clitheroe (pay-and-display), roadside parking at Brungerley Bridge
Refreshments	Food and drink is plentiful on this stretch, with cafés and/or pubs on or near the Ribble Way at Ribchester, Hurst Green, Mitton, Edisford Bridge and of course in Clitheroe
Toilets	By the car park in Ribchester, at Hurst Green, Clitheroe and Brungerley Bridge
Maps	OS Explorers 287, West Pennine Moors, and OL41, Forest of Bowland and Ribblesdale

For the next few miles the Ribble Way follows the river more closely, winding with it through a succession of lazy bends amid very attractive countryside. But there are also several distractions to delay your progress, the first being Ribchester itself, which has a fine church, a Roman museum and a village full of interesting buildings. At Stydd, just outside, is the oldest chapel in the Ribble valley and an intriguing suite of almshouses. Further on, having climbed away from the river above a bend, you might return briefly along the opposite bank to look at the Sale Wheel, a noted local beauty spot. Hurst Green, although no longer visited by the Ribble Way, is also worth a detour to see another splendid group of almshouses and nearby Stonyhurst College, where the historic house and beautiful gardens are opened to the public during the summer holidays. And if that is not attraction enough, the village is blessed with three pubs and lies on a bus route.

RIBCHESTER

Archaeologists tell us that the Romans were not the first to colonise the valley at Ribchester, as traces of a Bronze Age settlement have been discovered in the area, but it is the Roman presence for which the village is famous. Legionaries established a fort here in around 79 AD to guard a ford across the river at the intersection of the road north to Carlisle with another linking York and the west coast. To the Romans it was Bremetennacum, and although initially just a wooden structure protected by earthen banks, the defences were rebuilt in stone within 20 years.

Sadly, little now remains, much of the stone no doubt having been recycled over the centuries within the village, and in the 18th century a corner of the site was swept away when the river altered its course. However, the locations of several important buildings have been traced, including granaries and part of the headquarters complex. More substantial are the remains of the nearby baths, dating from around the time that the military

Map continues p.46

complex was rebuilt in stone. It is thought that they were used until around 225, though whether the buildings were subsequently demolished or merely abandoned is not clear. Excavations have revealed part of the hypercaust

45

Ribchester's Roman bath house

(heating system) and the outlines of the different hot and cold areas, including a circular room that housed a sauna. Archaeological finds around the baths and at the site of the fort include inscriptions, pottery, coins and even some ears of grain, but the greatest treasure, a splendid ceremonial helmet, was uncovered by chance in 1786 when the river undercut the fort. The one in the museum here is only a copy, as the original went to the British Museum. However, there are many other objects displayed, telling something of life in this far-flung corner of the Roman Empire.

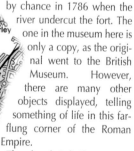

The church is built over part of the fort and dedicated to St Wilfrid. Born of noble blood in 634, Wilfrid journeyed to Rome, returning by way of Lyon where he became a monk, adopting the Roman rather than Celtic customs of Christianity. Wilfrid was appointed Bishop of York at the age of 30 and played a major part in establishing the Roman Church in England. ▶

The Roman excavations yielded evidence of early Christian symbols, and fragments of Celtic crosses have been found in the churchyard, but the first recorded date for the church is 1193 and the north doorway was possibly part of that building. The present nave and chancel are in the somewhat later style of Early English, about 1220, with the north chapel being added around the 14th century and the tower 100 years later. A glance from the outside shows that the roof was once much higher, and the unusual dormer windows were installed in 1712 to allow more light into the body of the building. Inside, the gallery was added in 1736 to accommodate musicians and a choir to lead the hymn singing. The pillars supporting it are optimistically credited as being Roman, but the nearby font is almost certainly Saxon. The 13th-century double piscina and triple sedilia are interesting features in the chancel, as is the hagioscope in the north wall. Often termed 'a lepers' squint', a hagioscope allows a view of the proceedings

Tradition has it that every church carrying St Wilfrid's dedication was actually founded by him, and if this is true then Ribchester's church lays claim to being one of the oldest in Lancashire.

St Wilfrid's Church at Ribchester

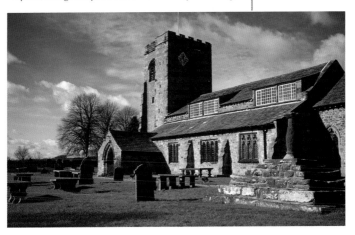

*The White Bull at
Ribchester*

at the altar from outside, a prudent precaution during
the Middle Ages, when leprosy was not uncommon
in the country.

Box pews were removed from many churches
during Victorian 'renovations', but a few remain
here, as well as the splendid 'cage' pew where sat
the Houghtons, one of the landed families of the
area. Another marvellous survivor is the 17th-century

pulpit, finely carved and complete with candle holders. Have a look, too, at the sundial as you pass through the churchyard. It is about 300 years old, but is mounted on the much older base of a medieval preaching cross.

After the departure of the Romans, Ribchester continued as an Anglo-Saxon settlement, but its prominence declined, perhaps aggravated by later Viking raids. The Norsemen were a seagoing race, and during the five centuries of the Dark Ages they harried much of Britain's northern coast and islands, taking what they could and always wreaking havoc. Although a good way inland, Ribchester was not immune. The Viking longships had a shallow draught that enabled them to navigate rivers and streams, often penetrating quite deeply into the hinterland.

Ribchester must afterwards have recovered to a position of some importance, for it received a mention in the Domesday survey, something not accorded to many places in Lancashire. But it suffered pillage again in 1332, this time at the hands of the Scots. Misfortune of a different kind struck in 1349 when the Black Death swept the land, claiming around half of Ribchester's population, many of whom lie in unmarked graves in the churchyard. Plague returned once more in the 17th century, but afterwards life for the inhabitants improved as flax and then cotton weaving developed as cottage industries. The sturdy 18th-century cottages of brick and stone imply a growing prosperity, many containing rooms with generous windows where the hand looms were installed. One of the village's most striking buildings is the White Bull, which has an upper room supported by Roman pillars that forms an impressive porch over the main entrance. Nearby is a mounting block, a relic of the days when most visitors arrived on horseback. However, as the 19th century began to unfold, the population of Ribchester again declined as the factory system enveloped textile production and drew people to the neighbouring

The Shireburn Almshouses at Stydd near Ribchester

towns, where the large mills were the main source of employment.

The Ribble Way skirts behind the primary school above the Ribble, then turns with Duddel Brook past the entrance of the second-century Roman bath house. Across a small green, follow the street right to the main road and continue past the Ribchester Arms and away from the village. Before crossing Stone Bridge, however, first wander up Stydd Lane for ¼ mile (400m) to see the Shireburn Almshouses and ancient St Saviour's Chapel.

STYDD

The almshouses at Stydd are named after their benefactor, Sir John Shireburn of Stonyhurst, and were constructed in 1728 for the relief of five Roman Catholic widows or spinsters. Grand in design yet tiny in scale, the elaborate Italianate facade makes these some of the most attractive buildings in the area. An elegant external flight of stairs rises to an ornately arcaded balcony from which doors lead to the upper apartments, although those below have less imposing entrances, tucked behind shaded porches on either side of the staircase. ▶

A little further along the lane is a tiny chapel dedicated to St Saviour, and thought to have been founded in 1136 during the reign of King Stephen. Credited with being the oldest extant chapel in the valley, it once formed part of a small monastic hospice. In the middle of the 13th century it was granted to the Knights Hospitallers, an order originally founded in the east during the crusades to provide succour to pilgrims making their way to the holy city of Jerusalem. The hospice's other buildings have long-since disappeared, but the chapel displays several fine features typical of Norman architecture: round-arched heads above door and window openings, and some bold zigzag decorative moulding over a blocked-up entrance in the north wall. There is also an unusual octagonal canopied pulpit from the Jacobean period, and an early 16th-century font bearing local heraldic emblems, while behind the screen is the grave of Frances Petre, a Roman Catholic bishop. That he was buried here, on Christmas Eve 1775, reflects the high

Towards the end of the last century the Shireburn Almshouses had become derelict, but have since been sympathetically restored and are again inhabited.

Leaving Dewhurst House

*Looking towards
Haugh Wood*

level of Catholic standing in the area at a time when
there was a great deal of religious prejudice and
persecution.

Returning to the main road, carry on to Ribchester
Bridge and remain on this bank along a track to
Dewhurst House. Walk into the farmyard and swing
right beside a barn, crossing a ladder stile at the back
to regain the water's edge. A quiet path follows the
Ribble upstream, passing below Stewart's Wood and on
into Haugh Wood. Approaching the far end of the trees,
move away from the river to a stile and then bear left
up a steep grass bank. Walk on over the hill, aiming for
the left-hand edge of Pendle Hill as it becomes visible,
and descend to a gate at the bottom of the dip. Carry on
to the top-left corner of the next field, then keep ahead
across a final enclosure to meet a track rising from Hey
Hurst farm. Through the gate opposite, follow the left
boundary downhill once more to find a bridge at the foot
of Clough Bank Wood. Wander on at the lower edge of
successive fields until the accompanying hedge eventually drops away. Now bear left to a gate in the upper
corner from which a rough track, joined part-way along
by a path from Dinckley Bridge, takes you on to Trough
House farm.

A sign points the way near Trough House

Pendle Hill from above Copy Scar Wood

THE SALE WHEEL

Although the riverbank below Trough House is a particularly pleasant stretch, the Ribble Way affords you little opportunity to see the river at close quarters. However, if you have time to spare, as you near Trough House, turn off to Dinckley Bridge and cross the Ribble, then follow it a little way back downstream into Marles Wood. Towards the western end of the wood bare rocky bergs narrow the valley and concentrate the flow of water, which swings abruptly to the right, swirling around in a deep dark pool known locally as the Sale Wheel.

Through the farm the track climbs away beside a wooded bank, soon reaching a stile on the right some 350 yards along.

HURST GREEN

At one time the Ribble Way climbed on along the track into Hurst Green, emerging onto the main road by the Shireburn Arms, then following the road all the way to Lower Hodder Bridge. Although now bypassed, Hurst Green remains a convenient

Dinckley Bridge

digression if you are looking for refreshment, accommodation or a bus, and it also has several sights worth
seeing. Hurst Green lies at the edge of Stonyhurst
Park, the one-time seat of the Shireburn family. Sir
John Shireburn was responsible for the almshouses
at Stydd, following the munificent example of his
forebear Sir Nicholas, who had established a suite
of 10 almshouses for his retired labourers at Kemple
End on Longridge Fell in 1706. By 1946 these buildings had become redundant, and were dismantled
and re-erected outside the entrance to Stonyhurst
Park at Hurst Green to serve as cottages for estate
workers there.

The almshouses at the entrance to Stonyhurst Park, Hurst Green

STONYHURST COLLEGE

At the centre of the park is Stonyhurst College, a splendid rambling building begun in 1523 by Hugh Shireburn, whose family had held the manor since the 12th century. His descendants greatly extended the house and landscaped the grounds. But following the untimely death in the 18th century of Richard Francis, the last male heir to the line, the property passed to the Welds, a Dorset family who, in 1794, offered it to the Jesuit College at Leige in Normandy. This college had originally been founded at St Omer in 1593 to provide an education for English Catholics at a time when they were suffering suppression at home under the Tudors. But times changed and during the 18th century the college experienced persecution at the hands of the French Revolution, being forced to move twice before finally coming to England. Alterations and new building have continued over the last 200 years to accommodate the college's expansion, most notably with the addition of the splendid Church of St Peter after the Act of Catholic Emancipation was passed in 1829.

In the 19th century the college established an enviable reputation for its scientific studies, and produced meteorological and astronomical data to an extremely high standard. As a result, two of the masters, Fathers Perry and Sidgreaves, were charged with making official observations of eclipses and other important events, including a transit of Venus during the 1870s. Shortly after, Gerard Manley Hopkins, the 19th-century poet, spent time there as a master – he had been ordained a priest in 1877. Among the school's many distinguished pupils have been Sir Arthur Conan Doyle, who used the setting of the college as a model for Baskerville Hall, and the actor Charles Laughton, remembered for his portrayals of Shakespearean characters as well as film parts such as Captain Bligh and Quasimodo. JRR Tolkien was a regular visitor – one of his sons undertook part of his training for the priesthood at St Mary's, and another son was a teacher at the college.

Stonyhurst College

It is said that the area around Stonyhurst was Tolkein's inspiration for Middle Earth in *The Lord of the Rings*.

You can visit the school and see some of the old classrooms, dormitories and the church, where among the treasures on display is its 40,000 volume library. The library contains a seventh-century copy of St John's Gospel, and the prayer book that Mary Queen of Scots took with her to her execution.

Guided tours take place during the summer holidays every afternoon except Friday between the middle of July and the August bank holiday, ending in the gardens, which are then at their most beautiful.

ROAD DEVELOPMENT

Hurst Green has another claim to fame, for at the end of the 19th century a section of the road through the village was one of the first in the country to be surfaced with 'quarrite'. This was a material developed in the limestone quarries at Trowbeck, near Silverdale in Lancashire, in which crushed roadstone was mixed with hot tar. As the automobile established itself as part of everyday life, dusty and muddy roads gradually became a thing of the past, and the promenade at Blackpool and the city streets of Edinburgh were among the earliest thoroughfares to benefit from this new process. Lancashire, incidentally, led the way in other aspects of road development, too – the first white lines to improve road safety appeared outside the Toll House Garage in Claughton, while the first stretch of motorway to be built in the country was the Preston bypass, opened on 5 December 1958 by the then prime minister, Harold Macmillan.

The Ribble Way now passes over the stile into the adjacent field, crossing to a second stile from which an undulating path skirts the top of the wooded bank above the river. When you eventually reach a stile on the left (marking a path across the fields into Hurst Green), turn away, dropping steeply through the trees to a bridge spanning Dean Brook at the bottom. The route continues at the edge of successive pastures beside the river. Shortly after passing a Water Board aqueduct, one of several crossing the Ribble, the way joins a track that goes by a house overlooking Jumbles Rocks, a low cataract briefly disturbing the smooth flow of the water. Keep following the river, which in a little while swings round in a tight bend as the River Calder joins through the far bank.

HACKING HALL

Over the water, Hacking Hall is a fine example of the kind of splendid country residence being built in the area at the beginning in 17th century. It is on the site of a very much older manor that was first mentioned in 1374 in connection with Whalley Abbey, and it was monks from there who constructed the nearby great tithe barn, which is supported by massive timber crucks. ▶

Behind the hedge on this side of the river is an even older relic – the massive mound in the middle of the field is a tumulus marking an ancient burial site.

The Ribble below Jumbles Rocks

HACKING BRIDGE

Draining the Forest of Rossendale, the Calder is a formidable river in its own right, and when the rivers are in spate the confluence presents a dramatic sight. Until its closure in 1954, the Hacking Ferry provided a convenient link between the paths on the separate shores, but in 1985, with no means of crossing here, the Ribble Way had to be routed north past the confluence with the Hodder (which emanates from Bowland in the north) to cross that river higher up at Lower Hodder Bridge. For 30 years, requests for a bridge to replace the ferry had remained unsatisfied, and although the opening of the Ribble Way provided a greater incentive to do something, funding remained a continuing problem. The new millennium brought fresh optimism and an innovative design was put forward for a unique triple-leg arch with a foot firmly planted on each of the three banks. A fibreglass-reinforced exoskeleton would be lifted into place by helicopter and then filled with concrete to create the finished bridge. But just as the dream was set to become reality, budget constraints once again came to the fore and the plan was shelved.

Carry on along the northern bank of the Ribble, eventually picking up a track that takes you past the river's confluence with the Hodder. Continue with it to Winckley Hall farm, winding left and right through the yard before leaving along a track that climbs away through the trees beyond. Go past the entrance to Winckley Hall at the top, but where the track then bends left, leave through a kissing gate on the right. Strike half-left across the fields, setting a course towards the distant spires of Stonyhurst College that appear on the horizon. Close with the right-hand fence in the second field to leave over a stile in the corner and carry on downhill at the edge of two more fields, emerging at a junction of lanes. Lower Hodder Bridge lies $^1/_3$ mile (500m) down to the right.

CROMWELL'S BRIDGE

Just below the road bridge is an ancient packhorse bridge, built in 1562 by Richard Shireburn. It is known locally as Cromwell's Bridge, for Cromwell supposedly took his army across to reach Stonyhurst in 1648. However, historians think it more likely that the force would merely have forded the river a little further downstream.

Continue beyond the bridge for a further 1/3 mile (500m) to a junction and go right, the way signed to Whalley. Alternatively, you can carry on for another 300 yards to the next turning and go right there, that lane being much quieter, yet incurring no appreciable extra distance. Both lanes lead to Great Mitton and meet by All Hallows Church opposite the Three Fishes. The route heads past the Hillcrest Tearoom, dropping steeply to the Ribble, where Mitton Bridge takes you across to the Aspinall Arms. The Ribble Way enters the field on the left immediately beyond it.

Cromwell's Bridge over the River Hodder

Across the valley to Wiswell Moor

ALL HALLOWS, GREAT MITTON

All Hallows at Great Mitton is one of the region's little gems, a splendid country church rich in history and containing many fine features. The wooden chancel screen is believed to have come from Sawley Abbey when the monks there were evicted during the dissolution of the monasteries, while the simplicity of the 14th-century font is offset by a beautifully carved pyramidal cover given to the church in 1593 by a local knight, Sir Richard Molyneux.

Have a wander around the churchyard before you leave, for in the southern section, which affords a grand prospect over the valley, is the carved head of a 14th-century cross.

The oldest part of the present building, the nave, dates from 1270, with the chancel being added 25 years later. However, records list rectors from the beginning of the 12th century, and substantiate a belief that there was an older church on the site, probably of wood and thatch, that perhaps went back to Saxon times.

The ancient cross at All Hallows Church

With the manner of Stonyhurst little over a mile away, it was the church to which the Shireburns looked, and in 1438 they added a family chapel onto the northern side of the chancel. Divided from the main body of the church by a splendid Elizabethan screen, it contains several beautifully carved tombs of alabaster and marble, while other family members lie in the crypt beneath. The earliest table tomb is of Sir Richard, who commissioned the rebuilding of the chapel in 1594. He is depicted recumbent in full armour beside his wife, Maude. He died in 1597 before the chapel was actually finished, the ill-matching roof-timbers over the windows implying a hasty completion to the work. On the floor nearby is a sandstone effigy of Sir Richard, much weathered, as it once lay outside in the churchyard. Later members of the family are grouped beneath the north wall, while to the side is a memorial to the last male of the Shireburn line, Richard Francis. He died tragically at the tender age of nine after eating poisonous berries, and with no successor the estate passed to the Welds. It was they who gave it to the Jesuits in France as a home for their school, and after crossing the Channel the priests apparently journeyed here on foot, accompanied by a small band of their pupils.

Follow the field perimeter around the side of the pub, rising along a high bank to continue above the water. Over a stile and then through a kissing gate, carry on parallel to the Ribble, crossing a small bridge over a side-stream before bearing left to regain the river's edge by a small building, a flood-level monitoring station. Beyond an aqueduct, carry on along a field track to Shuttleworth Farm, ultimately leaving the fields over a stile at the rear of the sheds. Through kissing gates, cross a small paddock and join the farm access road to walk away. Later parting company with the river and subsequently passing a small household waste reclamation site, the lane eventually leads to a bridge across a stream.

Looking ahead from Great Mitton

Over the bridge, turn off to Siddows Farm. Take the right fork where the track splits, however, then leave immediately through a kissing gate on the left. Cross to another gate in the opposite corner of the small field and then swing left, dropping through a hedged bank to continue by the river. Carry on at the edge of Edisford Park and climb out at the far end onto the road.

EDISFORD BRIDGE AND LOW MILL

An early crossing place of the river, Edisford is reputed to be the site of a battle between King Stephen and Scots raiders led by William Fitz Duncan.

The first bridge was built in the 14th century to replace the old ford that gave the place its name. Just upstream is the site of Low Mill, one of several textile mills that sprang up around Clitheroe as the mechanisation of the cotton industry gained pace. Established in 1782, it was powered by water taken from the river over ½ mile (800m) further upstream, the distance necessary to gain a sufficient head of water to work the banks of spinning frames and weaving looms. It prospered during the 19th century and a small village grew around it, complete with Methodist chapel and Sunday school. The mill was eventually converted to steam and continued operating until the 1950s, but was subsequently demolished and new housing rose on the site below the original mill village.

Head away from the bridge past the entrance of the Clitheroe Camping and Caravanning Club Site, crossing the road at pedestrian traffic lights to reach the leisure centre. Follow the main drive between the swimming pool and tennis hall, continuing across the playing field beyond. Curve round above the river, but towards the far end of the field bear right, emerging beside a retirement home onto a street in Low Moor village. Go left, remaining with the main street as it bends right past a junction, and then take the upper branch when it again divides. Keep ahead beyond the former Wesleyan Sunday school and the last of the houses, at which point the road degrades to a track. It leads between allotments and smallholdings before ending at some stables where a couple of kissing gates take you into the corner of a field. Climb away at the field edge to the crest of the hill, where there is a splendid view on the right to Clitheroe Castle. If you want to visit Clitheroe, you can either follow the path across the fields on the right to the edge of town, or continue to Brungerley Bridge and take the slightly longer route along the road. ▶

The Ribble Way to Brungerley Bridge carries on ahead, falling to the top of a steep wooded bank overlooking the river. Below is the weir for Low Mill at Edisford, a stepped path dropping to the riverbank above it. Carry on upstream, passing Waddow Hall on the opposite shore, which is now run as an activity and training centre by the Girl Guides' Association, and eventually emerging onto the road at Brungerley Bridge.

Clitheroe is the last town of any size before reaching Settle, but although close at hand, little of it is visible from the riverbank.

DAY WALKERS

A bus service between Clitheroe and Ribchester enables you to complete this leg one-way, and there are a number of possibilities for creating circular walks. A short walk can be had by crossing the river at Dinckley Bridge, returning to Ribchester via the De Tabley Arms, while a longer ramble leaves the Ribble Way after Trough House, climbing into Hurst Green from which several footpaths offer a choice of pleasant return routes across the rolling countryside. Alternatively, remain with the Ribble Way until it emerges onto the lane above Lower Hodder Bridge and circle back to Hurst Green by way of Stonyhurst College. From Brungerley Bridge, you can wander back on the other side of the river past Waddow Hall and then join the lane to Edisford. There, a permissive path, not shown on the map, follows the river to Fulshaw Wood, from which you can return to either Mitton or Lower Hodder Bridge.

CHAPTER 4

Brungerley Bridge to Gisburn Bridge

Distance	9.3 miles (15km)
Height gain	880 feet (268m)
Route assessment	Largely by riverside paths to Sawley, the path then climbs above Rainsber Gorge; a steep dip later brings a brief return to the water before rising again through fields to join a lane to Gisburn Bridge
Time	4½ hours
Public transport	There are bus services to Clitheroe and Gisburn; Clitheroe is also served by rail
Parking	Roadside parking at Brungerley Bridge and in Gisburn, but not at Gisburn Bridge itself
Refreshments	Clitheroe, Sawley and off the route at Gisburn
Toilets	At Brungerley Bridge and just off the A59 at Gisburn
Map	OS Explorer OL41, Forest of Bowland and Ribblesdale

Clitheroe is firmly Lancastrian, but before the reorganisation of local government in 1974 part of the boundary between Lancashire and Yorkshire followed the course of the Ribble. Between the confluence with the River Hodder and the point at which Swanside Beck meets the Ribble, a little way above Chatburn, the north bank was Yorkshire, a distance of about 7½ miles (12km) and a substantial section of the walk in fact. But with a bureaucratic sweep of the pen the boundary was shifted to the north and a vast tract of Bowland Forest suddenly became Lancashire, including the River Ribble as far as about 2 miles (3.2km) beyond Paythorne. Both counties are staunchly patriotic, and their traditional rivalry is passionately demonstrated in their support for their rugby and county cricket teams, yet, even though wars have been fought over less, the transition passed without major incident, and the only change you are likely to notice is in the style of markers beside the footpaths.

Oblivious to the new order, the onward river winds a pleasant course between a string of small villages set back on the rising valley sides. For the first part of this leg the Ribble Way follows the river quite closely, often shadowed by a similar path on the opposite bank, and even the extensive quarry workings north of Clitheroe have little impact on the beauty of this stretch of the river. Beyond Sawley the route strikes out onto the higher ground over Dockber, missing one of the prettiest stretches of the river, unfortunately, but offering some fine distant views in part compensation.

CLITHEROE

Clitheroe developed as a medieval market town. It grew around a strategically sited Norman castle begun by Roger de Poitou, the son of Roger de Montgomery who came over with William at the Conquest. But other than serving as a bastion against raiding Scots, the fortress saw little conflict during the medieval period and was used mainly as a centre for the administration of government and justice in the area. During the Civil War it was occupied as a Royalist stronghold, but in 1649, after the area was subjugated by the Parliamentarians following the Battle of Preston, the castle was largely demolished to prevent its re-use as a focus for resurgence. Only the ruined keep remains, a still impressive monument with walls over 9 feet (3m) thick, and attested to be the oldest building left in Lancashire. ▶

Local legend claims that the hole in its wall was made by the devil, who hurled a boulder from the Nick of Pendle, high up on the flanks of Pendle Hill, over 2½ miles (4km) away. More probably the damage was caused by Cromwell's cannons.

The castle now serves as the town's war memorial, and the attractive gardens surrounding it were laid out to celebrate the coronation of George VI in 1937. Within the grounds is the museum, located in 18th-century Castle House, which was built as a residence for the Steward of the Honour of Clitheroe.

Clitheroe's museum houses a fascinating exhibition on the geology of the area. Also on display is the ferry boat that used to ply between the river's banks at Hacking Hall.

Today's 'old' Clitheroe dates largely from the late 18th and 19th centuries. The church claims an early foundation – it is said that St Paulinus, sent as a missionary to Britain by Pope Gregory at the beginning of the seventh century, baptised converts in a nearby pool – but was substantially rebuilt in 1828, although below its more recent spire the tower and east window survive from an earlier building. Designed by the Victorian architect Rickman, his love of the Gothic style can be seen again at the Town Hall, which he decorated with the heraldry of old local families.

The town was instituted as a borough in 1147, during the reign of King Stephen, and is proud of its long history, one aspect of which is manifested in the mayor-making ceremonies. This ritual begins with a 'cockle and mussel feast' at which the town council chooses the mayor. On mayor-making day itself there is a procession of officials through the town, and in the evening a civic banquet is held at

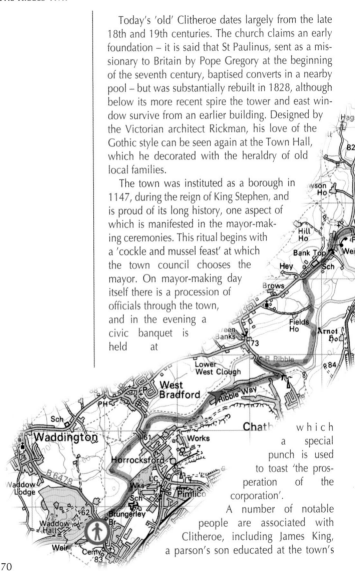

Chat which a special punch is used to toast 'the prosperation of the corporation'.

A number of notable people are associated with Clitheroe, including James King, a parson's son educated at the town's

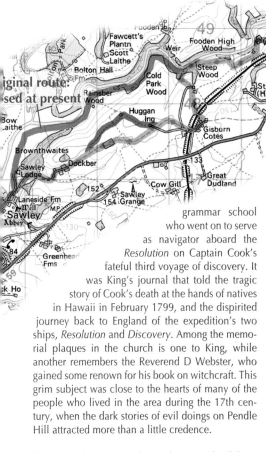

Map continues p.72

grammar school who went on to serve as navigator aboard the *Resolution* on Captain Cook's fateful third voyage of discovery. It was King's journal that told the tragic story of Cook's death at the hands of natives in Hawaii in February 1799, and the dispirited journey back to England of the expedition's two ships, *Resolution* and *Discovery*. Among the memorial plaques in the church is one to King, while another remembers the Reverend D Webster, who gained some renown for his book on witchcraft. This grim subject was close to the hearts of many of the people who lived in the area during the 17th century, when the dark stories of evil doings on Pendle Hill attracted more than a little credence.

Climb away from Brungerley Bridge towards Clitheroe, and after about 100 yards leave to the left into Brungerley Park. ▶

Choose the lower route where the path forks, and go left again when you subsequently reach a sign marking the Cross Hill Quarry Nature Reserve. Go over a stile and

There are a number of sculptures alongside the trail in Brungerley Park, and as you walk through, look out for a face peering from a trunk, and toadstools and strange seedpods scattered beneath the trees.

71

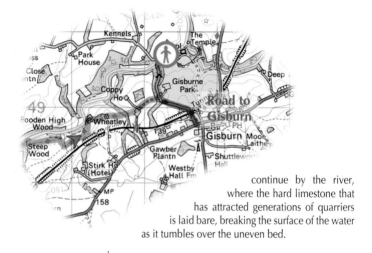

continue by the river, where the hard limestone that has attracted generations of quarriers is laid bare, breaking the surface of the water as it tumbles over the uneven bed.

CROSS HILL QUARRY

Limestone has long been a mainstay of Clitheroe's prosperity, the quarries being worked since at least the 17th century. Stone was cut for construction, or crushed and then burnt in kilns to produce lime. This versatile commodity was used as a fertiliser, in making building mortar, and in the iron smelting process. At one time it was taken out by teams of packhorses, with over 1000 loads leaving the quarries each day. However, the arrival of the railways enabled a dramatic increase in production, and with the development of tarmacadam as a road-surfacing material at the end of the 19th century, yet another insatiable market was found. Cross Hill Quarry was abandoned around 100 years ago, and lying undisturbed since then, has been reclaimed by nature. Birch, ash and hawthorn woodland has grown up, and in its shelter a surprising variety of plants has become established across the quarry floor and in the innumerable rocky crevices of the cliffs behind. ◄

Among the lime-loving plants that you might find are mouse-ear hawkweed, fairy flax, and sweet-smelling herbs such as wild thyme and marjoram.

72

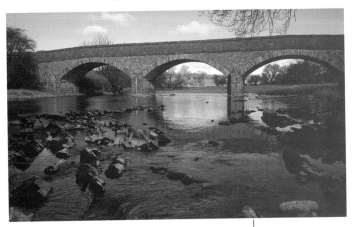

Bradford Bridge

These plants attract butterflies such as meadow browns, orange tips, common blues and painted ladies, which you will see fluttering their uncertain course from flower to flower throughout spring and into early autumn.

Keep a lookout for traffic coming from both directions when climbing down from the stile at Bradford Bridge, as it takes you straight onto a somewhat narrow section of road. Rejoin the riverbank through a kissing gate opposite and carry on upstream over occasional stiles, an agreeable, lightly wooded stretch of path, despite its proximity to a busy quarry. After a little over ¾ mile (1.2km), move away from the river to a stile that takes you onto the top of a beech-clad bank, the river below you sweeping to the north across the flat valley base. Later, leaving the wood, keep going at the edge of a field. The view on the right then opens to reveal Chatburn, strung out along a lane climbing out of the valley. It lies below the looming bulk of Pendle Hill, for so long a prominent landmark that has guided your forward progress, but to be left behind from now on. Trace the field boundary around to a kissing gate where you meet the lane and follow it left, back down to the river.

With time to spare on top of Pendle Hill

CHATBURN AND GRINDLETON

Lusty streams falling from the hills to the Ribble helped both Chatburn and Grindleton, its near neighbour across the river, to develop as textile producers. Water-powered cotton mills flourished for a time in both villages, and superseded an earlier hand-loom cottage industry. It was always known that the line of a Roman road from Skipton to Ribchester ran across the hillside just above Chatburn, but it still caused quite a stir when a cache of Roman coins was found near the village during the 19th century.

THE PENDLE WITCHES

There must be few people in England who do not associate Pendle Hill with tales of 17th-century witchcraft. At the centre of these stories are Old Demdyke and Mother Chattox, two ageing crones whose bickering families scratched a living by odd-jobbing and begging. After Alice Device, one of Old Demdyke's brood, was charged with casting a spell on a travelling peddler who later died in an apoplectic fit, suspicion spread as the two feuding families hurled ever-more spiteful accusations at each other. Even one of the gentry class, Alice Nutter of Roughlee, was dragged into the affair, with allegations that she was a party to the Demdykes' sorcery and had profited thereby in calling upon the dark forces to magically further her case in a land dispute. In the end five of them, as well as Alice Nutter, were found guilty and hanged at Lancaster Castle. Only Old Demdyke escaped the grisly punishment, having died before the trial began.

Attentive walkers will notice that as the lane accompanies the river, they are apparently going the wrong way, downstream, but this anomaly is necessary in order to gain the opposite bank at Grindleton Bridge. ▶

Swing sharp right over the bridge to join a riverside path, passing the outflow of Swanside Beck some ¾ mile (1.2km) upstream, which used to mark the old Lancashire boundary. Just after the confluence cross a stile and walk away from the bank to a second stile, then bear right up the field to a ladder stile beyond a stream at the far end. Climb away above an abrupt fold

Upstream of Grindleton Bridge, the river has undercut the bank, taking with it the path, and although reinstatement is planned, it has not yet been completed. In the meantime, a diversion is signed along the lane via Grindleton village to Sawley.

The Ribble below Grindleton Bridge

Approaching Sawley Bridge

containing the stream and, after negotiating another stile at the top, strike diagonally across to a final stile to the left of a gate in the top wall out of the field. Follow the lane right, cresting the hill to drop into Sawley. Approaching the village you can avoid the last section of lane down to the bridge by crossing into the meadow beside the water. Rejoining the lane, walk over the bridge into Sawley.

CLOSURE OF THE ORIGINAL FOOTPATH AT SAWLEY

When the Ribble Way was first established it followed the river north from Sawley into a beautiful wooded gorge. Unfortunately, not long after the path opened the landowner successfully contested the legal standing of the bridleway passing through his property, and in 1999 it was closed, with the way being diverted along the hillside overlooking the valley. There is always hope that the path may eventually be reopened, and that walkers will once again be able to enjoy the splendid seclusion of this fine stretch. However, in the meantime you must follow the high-level route.

Before leaving Sawley have a look at the remains of Sawley Abbey, which lie a short distance to the right from the junction by the Spread Eagle.

SAWLEY ABBEY

A Cistercian house, Sawley Abbey was founded in 1147 by 12 monks from Fountains Abbey, at Ripon, on land given to them by the third Baron Percy. Lacking the rich resources surrounding its mother church, Sawley was never a wealthy community, yet the excavated foundations and the humps and hollows in the nearby fields suggest extensive buildings, gardens and fishponds, and imply that it enjoyed reasonable prosperity during the 400 years before it was

The 'ancient arch' at Sawley

closed during the dissolution of the monasteries. Its last abbot bravely voiced dissent against Henry VIII's government of the country and resolved to wrest the Church from the control of Rome, joining the Pilgrimage of Grace in 1536. But the northern rebellion collapsed and the abbot was tried for treason at Lancaster Castle. Found guilty, he was executed there in 1537, while the small band of monks once under his care were evicted and left to make the best way they could in the outside world.

The surviving ruins are perhaps visually less impressive than some of the great religious houses lying further to the east, and much of the stone has been taken for re-use in other buildings. An odd example of this cannibalisation is the striking archway beside the road, one of two that were built from the stones lying among the crumbling walls. They were erected to enhance the romantic lure of the ruins when the village developed a reputation as a local beauty and picnic spot during the 19th century, and old pictures show them to have been set in tandem across the road, creating the impression of an ancient gateway into the abbey precincts. However, they proved too narrow to accommodate the later arrival of motorised traffic, and after several accidents occurred, were eventually demolished. One arch was subsequently resurrected out of the way in the adjacent field, but it now looks somewhat incongruous in relation to the rest of the ruins. ◀

Hoary vaulting encasing the cellars below the Spread Eagle is authentic looking, and suggests that it was originally part of the abbey complex. This building's history is certainly ancient, and it is known to have served as an inn since the 16th century.

Return to the Spread Eagle and follow the minor lane forward beside the river to a bend, there passing through a gateway along the drive towards Sawley Lodge. It is from here that the Ribble Way was diverted in 1999, and if the original line of the route ever reopens, notices reminding ramblers of the closure will be removed. Until such a time walkers must leave the drive after 150 yards through a narrow gate on the right. Climb to the track above and follow it left, eventually winding up through West Dockber Farm.

Continue climbing beyond, the track shortly ending through a gate at the top. Pass through a second gate on the right and bear left towards the bottom corner of a plantation. Over a stile by the ruins of a stone building, walk forward to another stile on the right, and turn left at the edge of the trees. Keep going beyond the end of the trees to gates near the next field corner, passing through to strike a left diagonal. After another gate, carry on now with a fence on your right, maintaining your direction beside a line of outgrown hawthorn bushes to emerge on a track beside a farm, Huggan Ing. Cross to a stile, opposite to the right, and continue beside an old field boundary.

ALTERNATIVE ROUTE

An alternative route lies over a stile on the left, about 300 yards along the track climbing away from West Dockber Farm. It offers a fine prospect over the secluded valley where the Ribble Way originally ran, looking across to Rainsber Scar and the fringe of the Bowland Hills beyond. In the field, bear right across the corner to a gate and then keep ahead along the shallow crest of the ridge. Shortly you will reach the roofless ruin of Dockber Laithe. Immediately past the barn, wind through a gate and follow the fence right to a stile. Strike half-right, passing the marshy pond of Ox Hey Well, and maintain the same line beyond to the farm at Huggan Ing. Mounting a stile to the right of the barns, circle around to a second stile. Over this, join a track leaving to the right. However, just a few yards along climb a stile on the left and rejoin the line of the Ribble Way beside an old boundary.

THE PUDSAY FAMILY OF BOLTON HALL

Until it was demolished during the last century, Bolton Hall stood on the northern bank of the Ribble in the crook of land contained by its confluence with Skirden Beck. It was the home of the Pudsay family, of whom William attained some notoriety through incurring the wrath of Queen Elizabeth I. Her spies discovered that he was minting his own money, perhaps a not unreasonable expedient in his own eyes as he attempted to extricate himself from impending bankruptcy. The silver used was from his own mine at nearby Rimington, but nevertheless she dispatched a force to arrest him. In fleeing on horseback as his pursuers arrived, he is credited with clearing the width of the Ribble in a single leap from the top of Rainsber Scar. If true, it was certainly a monumental bound, and the memory of the event lives on in the name of the spot, Pudsay's Leap.

His ancestor, Sir Ralph, gained a prodigious reputation in another direction, and is depicted lying in full armour above his tomb in the church at Bolton-by-Bowland. Beside him are his three wives: on his right, Matilda Tempest, and beside her Margaret Tunstall, while on the other side is Edwina, who surprisingly managed to survive her husband, as the wives bore him two, six and 17 children respectively. All 25 are pictured, with their names, in three registers below their parents' feet. Unlike his descendant, Sir Ralph curried favour with his monarch, sheltering Henry VI, who was by then a lost cause following the Lancastrian defeat at Hexham in Northumbria during the Wars of the Roses in 1464.

Over the next stile take a diagonal line to another farm, Gisburn Cotes Hall, emerging through a gate in the corner of the field at a junction of tracks. Bearing left, walk past the front of the farmhouse and over a railway bridge. Where the track then forks, go left to Gisburn Cotes Farm.

In the yard, pass through a gate on the left and head back to the railway. Over the bridge, swing right towards another farm, crossing stiles on its left to emerge onto a track. Signed left to Fooden Ford, follow it through a dip to a bend, there leaving over a stile in front. Accompany the fence down to the head of a wooded gully, crossing another stile to continue on a stepped path that drops steeply to the Ribble. Meeting the riverbank at the ford, the route now rejoins the original line of the Ribble Way.

Lambing time at New Laithe near Gisburn

A short distance upstream, over a stile, veer away onto a rising track along the valley side. After winding above the head of a side-stream, at the field edge the way resumes its heading to an isolated barn, New Laithe. Dogleg right and left around it to continue in the adjacent field and leave over a final stile onto a drive. Heading away from a cottage, the route rises to a group of farm buildings. Turn off, mounting a stile beside a gate on the left just before reaching the buildings and strike out over the crest of the field, dropping to a small gate in the far fence. A trod leads up to a bridge spanning a stream. Climb through the trees beyond into a field and there bear right to Coppice Farm. Through the yard, a track to the left joins the drive from Copy House, eventually taking you out to a lane. Gisburn, where you will find accommodation and refreshment, lies ½ mile (800m) to the right, while the onward Ribble Way follows the lane downhill to the river and Gisburn Bridge.

DAY WALKERS

The linear walk is facilitated by a bus service between Gisburn and Clitheroe; simply follow the lane up from Gisburn Bridge at the end of the walk to meet the A59 in the town, where in the morning you will have found a place to park and the bus stop. Alternatively, you can break the section into two circular walks. Footpaths follow the northern bank of the river for much of the way between Sawley and Brungerley Bridge, while there are a couple of possibilities from Gisburn Bridge. One of these takes you through Bolton-by-Bowland, where the 13th-century church is of interest and refreshment is provided by both a pub and a tea room. The other leads past Bolton Hall Farm, but if you choose this route, note that the path west from Bolton Hall to Skirden Beck is no longer as depicted on the Ordnance Survey map. It now runs a little further to the north, following the line of an old track to a ford where a bridge provides a dry-shod crossing to pick up the path from Bolton-by-Bowland to Sawley.

CHAPTER 5

Gisburn Bridge to Settle

Distance	12 miles (19.3km)
Height gain	780 feet (238m)
Route assessment	The route undulates over open rolling hills and moorland at the fringes of the valley, where the way may be boggy in places, finally joining the riverbank for the last stretch into Settle
Time	5½ hours
Public transport	Bus travel between Settle (where there is also a railway station) and Gisburn is via Skipton; services also run through Wigglesworth and Rathmell from Settle
Parking	Roadside parking in Gisburn (but not at Gisburn Bridge) and pay-and-display car parks at Settle
Refreshments	At Gisburn, Paythorne and in Settle with a pub close to the route at Wigglesworth
Toilets	Just off the A59 at Gisburn and beside car park at Settle
Map	OS Explorer OL41, Forest of Bowland and Ribblesdale

Although now bypassed by the long-distance walk, Gisburn is still a convenient break point, offering accommodation and refreshment at the White Bull and served by public transport. However, the route itself follows a pleasant path through Gisburne Park below the town, and subsequently avoids the busy A682 by using a new path created in the bordering field. Beyond Paythorne the nature of the country-side changes once more as the slopes enclosing the valley move back, leaving the river to pick its own course across the base of a broad, flat vale. At last, on Paythorne Moor, you enter Yorkshire, and the map calls it Ribblesdale, but you are still some way from 'the Dales' themselves. Their hills rise in the distance, and as did Pendle before, the far-off summits of Pen-y-ghent and Ingleborough now appear as landmarks by which to reckon forward progress. Closer to, however, the hillsides are green and gently rolling, with field boundaries tending to be drystone wall rather than hedge, and occasional copses and coverts contributing to the neat, pastoral landscape melange. Once more the way inclines away from the river in favour of the higher ground and softly undulating moorland, and on consideration it is perhaps no bad thing. There is a lack of waterside footpaths, yes, but the uncertain course plotted by the river further upstream means marshy pastures that are potentially heavy going in anything but the driest weather. On the other hand, the elevation offers panoramas and an undulating terrain that add to the anticipation of what lies ahead.

Immediately before reaching Gisburn Bridge, turn off sharp right onto a bridleway, following it left beside some buildings and then up between wooded banks to stables. Keep with it to the right, winding across the grounds in front of a large house, Gisburne Park, now a private hospital. At a junction of tracks, cross the main drive and drop into a wooded valley surrounding Stocks Beck. Over a stone bridge the way bends right to a fork. Bear left and then left again past a lodge to climb away. Leave the wood at the top and continue along the track across the fields to the A682.

GISBURN

A century after founding Sawley Abbey, the Percys extended their pious gift with a further grant of land, the manor of Gisburne, to the abbot. After the dissolution of the monasteries the estate was acquired by the Lister family, who fostered the development of the town as an important market centre, a tradition continuing today in its regular livestock markets. Its 17th–19th-century buildings also reflect the town's importance as a staging post, and the Ribblesdale Arms was built to accommodate the coach trade passing through. The Lister family built the fine hall in the park in 1724, and strengthened their position in the county when Thomas Lister was raised to the peerage in 1797.

Map continues p.86

The title Baron Ribblesdale of Gisburne Park was Thomas Lister's reward for raising a force to defend the country in the face of the threat from the Napoleonic armies.

Among Baron Ribblesdale's other holdings was land around Malham, just over the hill behind Settle, on which he let the lucrative mining rights for calamine, a zinc ore used with copper for the production of brass, and ochre, a colorant in making paint. As a base for his frequent visits, Lister built Tarn House overlooking Malham Tarn, later lived in by Walter Morrison, whose friend John Ruskin was a regular guest there. Another visitor to the house was Charles Kingsley, who took from it the inspiration for his moralising fantasy *The Water Babies*. The Ribblesdale title died out in 1925 with the death of the fourth lord, although the name lived on for a time in the Ribblesdale Arms, but that too has now gone.

Gisburn's surviving pub, the White Bull, recalls the wild white cattle that used to roam the estate, but unlike those at Chillingham in Northumberland the herd dwindled and the last bull died in 1859.

The railway arrived at Gisburn in 1885, and it is said that railway officialdom was responsible for changing the spelling of the town's name, since omitting the 'e' would save the clerks many hours each year writing out the station's name. Whether or not the story

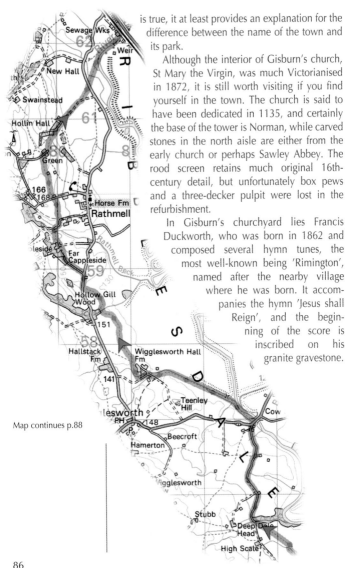

is true, it at least provides an explanation for the difference between the name of the town and its park.

Although the interior of Gisburn's church, St Mary the Virgin, was much Victorianised in 1872, it is still worth visiting if you find yourself in the town. The church is said to have been dedicated in 1135, and certainly the base of the tower is Norman, while carved stones in the north aisle are either from the early church or perhaps Sawley Abbey. The rood screen retains much original 16th-century detail, but unfortunately box pews and a three-decker pulpit were lost in the refurbishment.

In Gisburn's churchyard lies Francis Duckworth, who was born in 1862 and composed several hymn tunes, the most well-known being 'Rimington', named after the nearby village where he was born. It accompanies the hymn 'Jesus shall Reign', and the beginning of the score is inscribed on his granite gravestone.

Map continues p.88

The path strikes across the fields to Castle Haugh

Also in the churchyard is a wrought-iron slab bearing a relief which some say depicts a woman with a cauldron. Legend has it that it is a memorial to Jennet Preston, accused but subsequently acquitted of murdering a baby of the Lister family. Unluckily for her, Martin Lister, who had led the prosecution, died shortly after the trial and Jennet was hanged for witchcraft. But the link is somewhat flawed, for as a witch she would not have been buried in consecrated ground, and the monument is more likely to be from the 19th century, representing a cherub and urn.

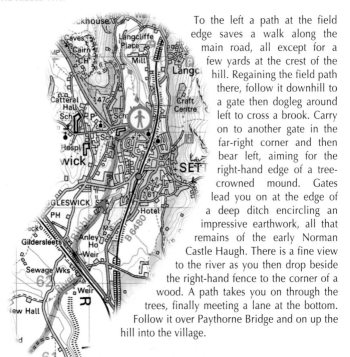

To the left a path at the field edge saves a walk along the main road, all except for a few yards at the crest of the hill. Regaining the field path there, follow it downhill to a gate then dogleg around left to cross a brook. Carry on to another gate in the far-right corner and then bear left, aiming for the right-hand edge of a tree-crowned mound. Gates lead you on at the edge of a deep ditch encircling an impressive earthwork, all that remains of the early Norman Castle Haugh. There is a fine view to the river as you then drop beside the right-hand fence to the corner of a wood. A path takes you on through the trees, finally meeting a lane at the bottom. Follow it over Paythorne Bridge and on up the hill into the village.

SALMON SUNDAY

The third Sunday of November is known locally as Salmon Sunday, and around that time you can expect to see salmon fighting their way upriver beneath the bridge to spawn in the higher reaches of the Ribble. The fish spend the first three years of their life in its clear streams before following the river down to the sea where they disperse across the northern Atlantic. When fully mature, some instinct prompts them to return to freshwater to breed, almost miraculously guiding them to the very stream in which they hatched, and so continues the cycle in producing the next generation.

A winter's day near Paythorne

Approaching the Dales, laithes (field barns) become a common sight

Leave the lane onto a track opposite the Buck Inn, Paa Lane, and follow it past Manor House Farm to a laithe (a field barn). There, cross left to a gate at the beginning of an old sunken grassy track. Higher up, as it bends right, ignore the gated track off to the left and carry on by the field edge, the way shortly developing as another abandoned track, Ing Lane. Where it eventually swings right into the corner of a field, keep ahead through a gate and over a stream. Mounting the stile in front, bear left to a gate in the shallow corner and then right through a second gate. A good path curves away across rough pasture, soon reaching a ditch crossing. Leave there, following the ditch right down to a footbridge spanning Ged Beck. Accompany it downstream to re-cross at a second footbridge, then aim just right of a solitary tree to cross a broken wall. Now back in pasture, carry on, passing a post marking a span over an intervening ditch to a gate. Cross a final field to emerge onto a lane.

Turn right towards Town End Farm, but then go off left immediately before it onto a track, Brook Lane. Stay ahead past a junction to reach Low Scales Farm, but on approaching its gate go over a stile to the left and skirt around the cottage boundary. Rejoin the line of the track at the far side and carry on past a lone barn, Middle Laithe. Keep going beside a ditch to a stile, cross to a second stile on the right and then walk left. When the fence later curves away, maintain your direction to a stile by a gate and cross to the far corner of the next field to meet a track from High Scale Farm. Going forward, it leads across the head of a wooded clough, Deep Dale, before winding across the fields to end at a lane above Cow Bridge.

A bridge over Ged Brook

HELLIFIELD

Looking over the valley from the high ground, the view is across the Ribble to Hellifield. This village grew around the railway junction where the route from Lancashire joined the LMS line, passing Settle to head north across the watershed into the Eden valley and on to Carlisle. The station opened in 1880 and the junction was busy for almost 100 years, but it eventually followed the rest of the railway system into decline during the 1960s. The revival of the Settle-to-Carlisle service, however, brought a new lease of life, and the station, which has fine cast-iron-and-glass canopies above the platforms, was restored to its former glory in 1994.

LONG PRESTON

The lane across Cow Bridge leads to the appropriately named village of Long Preston, strung out along the main road for almost ¾ mile (1.2km). ◄

Near the village green is the church. It too appears long, the effect emphasised by the squat tower at its western end and a low-pitched roof. Inside is a striking font sheltering beneath a massive 18th-century lantern cover, while on the walls above are hung charity boards cataloguing bequests to the church and local poor. One endowment funded a yearly sermon in perpetuity, while several others supported the Long Preston Hospital, a group of almshouses founded in 1613 that stand beside a bridge where the A682 crosses the railway south of the village.

Drop towards Cow Bridge, a low, drawn-out structure, its central span flanked by triple side arches to accommodate the river in full spate. Turn off immediately before it and head upstream to a stile at the top of the narrowing field. After making this brief encounter with the Ribble, the route once more turns away and instead

Long Preston village green has one of the country's surviving maypoles, and is the focus of festivities at the traditional start of spring, helped along no doubt with refreshments from the Maypole Inn opposite.

follows Wigglesworth Beck, here disciplined within an unnaturally straight course. ▶

Elaborate drainage and restraining dykes have claimed a large acreage from the winter flood meads, but even so, many of the fields remain quite marshy. Keep walking beside the stream on this bank until you reach a junction of tracks in front of a cottage at Wigglesworth Hall Farm.

Go right and right again across the beck to follow a track out to the left. After crossing a cattle-grid, bear off right over a stream and walk directly away, parallel to the boundary on the right. Negotiating a stile next to a gate, advance past a power-cable post and over the rise of the field, leaving near the right-hand corner to join a fenced track. To the left it leads on across the fields, with both Ingleborough and Pen-y-ghent beckoning from the distance. When the track shortly forks, keep directly ahead, splitting the angle to climb the field to a stile. Carry on by a wall and then, through a gate, swing left with the line of a fence above a deepening valley. Reaching a wall bounding a wood, drop to a bridge and double back downstream for 20 yards before striking up the bank to a stile in the top fence. Stride away with the fence on your left, and after crossing another stile, curve left as the narrowing enclosure ushers you out onto a lane.

Notice that the field drain on the left of Wigglesworth Beck is considerably deeper than the beck itself and, most unusually, a little further on the drain turns beneath a small aqueduct to pass under the stream.

Beyond Wigglesworth to Gisburn Forest

Walk 200 yards to the right, then leave opposite a barn along a track to Far Cappleside Farm. Just before it bends left at the end of the buildings, find a stile on the right and cross a small paddock to another stile in the corner. Carry on below Cappleside, an early 19th-century country house that looks out across the park, and meeting the main drive, keep walking ahead past stables and outbuildings. At the end by a large shed, drop forward into a dip where a gate guards an ancient packhorse bridge spanning Rathmell Beck.

On the far side a stony track climbs right to a gate behind Layhead Farm. Go left, but as the track then swings right, take the second left through a gate onto a narrow sunken track that is waymarked as a bridleway. Sadly, you only stay with this idyllic old lane for about 20 yards before climbing through the hedge bank on the right to a stile. Carry on along the boundary into the next field and over another stile, but where the wall then moves away, bear left across the field to come out onto a lane opposite Rathmell's school. Be careful, for the path drops straight onto the carriageway.

The village lies just down the hill, but the onward way is to the left, where some 30 yards along you will find a stile on the right. Skirt a small playing field to reach a kissing gate and continue at the edge of successive fields past a barn, eventually emerging onto a track beside cottages at Green. Turn right between the buildings to the end of a track, and through a gate there head downhill towards a farm at the bottom, Hollin Hall. Leave the field over a stile behind the barn and walk through to the small yard. Go right and then fork left to leave along a track. Where it later curves right, bear off left to a stile and cut the field corner to reach the road.

Diagonally opposite, another stile takes you back into the fields. Maintain the same course, crossing a slab bridge spanning a small stream in the middle, to a stile in the curving boundary ahead. Carry on around the head of another brook to join the riverbank. The way once more follows the Ribble upstream, shortly passing beneath the railway line and A65 trunk road. Ahead to the right is Settle, while opposite on this bank is the smaller village of Giggleswick, the cupola atop the chapel of its famous school rising as a landmark. Beyond Brigholme Barn the field narrows to a gate and stile beside a bend in the river. Through that, head away towards houses, passing through a gate onto Station Road, but take care, as there is no footway.

Cross to a footpath amid the bungalows opposite, which leads to a small estate behind. Join the street only as far as the next bend, there leaving right on another

Leave the river to have a look at old Giggleswick

Despite being overshadowed by a housing estate on one side and the back of industrial buildings on the other, the river here is quite dramatic, tumbling as a lively waterfall over a rugged step of limestone, the first cascade of any note so far encountered in your trek from the sea.

footpath between houses leading back to the river. A contained path conducts you along the edge of the playing fields of Giggleswick School, carrying on beyond them beside the river. A footbridge reached a little further along is a memorial to the servicemen of Giggleswick who gave their lives in two world wars. ◀

The centre of old Giggleswick, worthy of exploration, can be found just behind the houses on the left, and the path leading away from the bridge provides the shortest route to it. The Ribble Way, however, remains on the riverside path, which soon ends at the road by the old Settle Bridge. The town centre lies up to the right, while the onward route into upper Ribblesdale continues along a path between the playing fields on the far side of the road.

GIGGLESWICK

The suffix 'wick' betrays a Norse influence on Giggleswick, the result of Danish settlers finding their way into the higher reaches of the Ribble valley.

Nestling in the shelter of a dramatic limestone scar, part of the South Craven Fault, the ancient heart of the settlement around the church and Tems Beck is particularly attractive. A Saxon foundation, the church is one of only two in the country dedicated to Saint Alkelda, the other being not that far away at Middleham in Wensleydale. According to legend, Alkelda was a ninth-century Saxon princess who was put to death by strangulation for maintaining her faith in defiance of the pagan Norse invaders. Her appointed executioners were two women. The church incorporates stone from earlier buildings, one of which was destroyed in the early 14th century by a band of Scots marauders. The present structure, however, dates from around the 15th century and is a 'typical' Dales church, if there can be said to be such a thing. It is long and low with a modest squat tower, and the nave flows straight into the chancel. There is some especially fine woodwork from the 17th century inside, particularly the pulpit and communion rail.

Giggleswick's well-known public school stands above the village, its distinctive cupola-topped chapel a landmark for miles around. It was founded in 1507 on land near the church granted to the chantry priest, James Carr, and subsequently given a royal charter by Edward VI in 1553. In 1867 it moved to a larger site at the top of the hill where, in 1897, work began on a chapel to celebrate Queen Victoria's golden jubilee. It was the gift of Walter Morrison, a governor of the school and local benefactor who, as mentioned earlier in this chapter, lived at Tarn House overlooking Malham Tarn. He wanted a building that was in total harmony with its setting and complete in every detail so that there would be no opportunity for future additions or alterations that might detract from its integral beauty.

The Astronomer
Royal came to
Giggleswick School
in 1927 to view the
solar eclipse of that
year.

Designed by T G Jackson, the chapel was completed
in 1901, the year of the queen's death, and is a magnificent example of religious Gothic art. If you want
to have a look, it is open to the public during the
day on weekdays. The school itself has an outstanding reputation, boasting several distinguished former
pupils, and like the college at Stonyhurst, has a well-
equipped observatory. ◄

DAY WALKERS

Most people would find this section in its entirety too long for a circular
walk, but it can be conveniently split into more manageable proportions
at Paythorne and Cow Bridge near Wigglesworth, where unlike Gisburn
Bridge, you will be able to park at the roadside. A pleasant route lies via
Moor House Farm between Paythorne and Gisburn Bridges, whilst there
is a choice of returning along the middle section by way of Thornbar or
above Tosside Beck, dependant upon how long you want to make the day.
To get back to Cow Bridge from Settle, the most direct route is across the
high ground overlooking the eastern side of the valley to Long Preston, but
the maze of paths across the rolling hills to the west of the Ribble Way
offer other possibilities. Public transport is an alternative, with the Bowland
Transit service from Settle running through Rathmell and Wigglesworth. It is
also possible to travel between Settle and Gisburn, but you need to change
at Skipton. The best plan here is to leave your car in Settle and catch the
early morning train (at the time of writing 7.31am) to Skipton. A 45-minute
wait for the bus gives you time for a spot of breakfast, and you should then
be in Gisburn shortly after 9.30, giving ample time to complete the walk.
Gisburn Bridge lies ¾ mile (1.2km) from the town, along a narrow lane
leaving the A59 by the cattle market and former station.

CHAPTER 6

Settle to Horton in Ribblesdale

Distance	7.5 miles (12km)
Height gain	980 feet (299m)
Route assessment	Initially following the river, the track later climbs through hillside pastures onto the fringe of the eastern moors, returning to the river on its opposite bank for the last part of the stage into Horton
Time	3¾ hours
Public transport	Rail link between Settle and Horton in Ribblesdale
Parking	Car parks in Settle and Horton in Ribblesdale (pay-and-display)
Refreshments	A choice of cafés and pubs in both Settle and Horton in Ribblesdale, also pubs beside the route at Stainforth and Helwith Bridge
Toilets	In Settle, Stainforth and Horton in Ribblesdale
Maps	OS Explorers OL41, Forest of Bowland and Ribblesdale, and OL2, Yorkshire Dales (Southern & Western areas)

Settle lies at the edge of the Yorkshire Dales National Park, one of the country's most popular walking areas. The hills, up until now seen only from afar, quickly close around the valley and usher you into true Dales country. Below the town the broad, flat-bottomed vale of the Ribble rapidly dwindles to a relatively narrow gap, its encompassing slopes rising ever more bluntly on either side. Yet for a time at least the valley retains its gentle pastoral charm, a patchwork of lush woodland and bright-green riverside fields. As the surrounding hills close upon the valley, the path's ascents become increasingly purposeful, but in compensation the scenery becomes more dramatic as you progress up the valley. However, unlike some of the neighbouring dales, upper Ribblesdale is not remote and untouched, because along its length run a road and a railway. This ready accessibility left the dale vulnerable to economic exploitation, and the removal of its profitable limestone and slate quickly assumed industrial proportions. The quarries still operate, creating raw, sharp cliffs in the weather-worn hillside, but there is much more, not least the natural scars, pavements, caves, pots and resurgences (underground streams that break to the surface) of limestone country all around, to catch the eye and distract you from man's activity. But before you carry on up the valley, have a look at Settle.

Settle and its close neighbour Giggleswick lie beneath the junction of the South and Mid Craven Faults. This great uplift of land occurred some 30 million years ago, raising the limestone that had been laid down in shallow tropical seas around 300 million years ago. These dramatic cliffs form a natural geological boundary to the northwest, while to the east the scar continues across higher ground to culminate in its most impressive displays at Malham Cove and Gordale Scar. Settle nestles at the edge of a rugged, alien landscape that instilled feelings of awe in Victorian travellers, and for Defoe, who passed this way in 1724, the land was 'nothing but high mountains which had a terrible aspect'.

SETTLE

Settle developed as a market on an ancient track linking Cumbria and Yorkshire, attracting wool from the monastic sheep-runs to the north and agricultural produce from the lower-lying farms in the south. ◄

Granted a charter under Henry III in 1249, the market is still held at Settle every Tuesday.

Settle has always been relatively prosperous, but things really took off in 1753 when a turnpike was built between Keighley and Kendal. Its several inns expanded to satisfy the increased trade, with some even relocating to attract the passing traffic. Much of the old part of the town dates from that period, with comfortable houses developing around courts and yards, and workshops springing up which undertook all manner of business. A further impetus to the industry of the town came with the construction of the Leeds and Liverpool Canal, which passed through Gargrave, less than 10 miles (16.1km) away. The powerful stream of the Ribble had long been used to drive mills, but with effective and cheap transport suddenly close at hand, the mills were enlarged and turned to cotton manufacture, a very lucrative business in those early days when British influence and trade across the world was growing fast.

Map continues p.103

A frequent visitor to Settle was Sir Edward Elgar, who stayed in a house belonging to his friend, Dr Buck, overlooking the square. Like the visitor of today, he must have been struck by the contrast between the busy-ness and back-street tranquillity to be found in the town. It is a place full of nooks and crannies as well as many fine buildings, of which the 17th-century Shambles overlooking the market place is a good example, although the upper storey was added somewhat later. One of the town's most impressive buildings is even older, and lies on a street a little further back. It is a lavishly elegant house from 1675, the whole frontage a splendid display of mullioned windows, a statement of affluence and the status symbol of its day. Known variously as Tanner Hall or Richard's Folly, it was built for a wealthy local tanner, Richard Preston, but his extravagance cost him dear, for he ran out of money before the house was finished. Many of Settle's buildings carry date stones and inscriptions above their doorways, but none is more unusual than that found on the wall of Ye Olde Naked Man facing the market place. Now a bakery and café, it was formerly an inn, and the emblem of a naked man modestly clutching a plaque dated 1663 in front of him was a satirical comment on the ostentatiously elaborate fashions of the day.

Richard's Folly now houses the Museum of North Craven Life

If you are there in summer, have a look at the Museum of North Craven Life located in Richard Preston's wonderful house. Unfortunately it has only limited opening times, so check with the tourist information office, but the interesting displays on local themes are as diverse as the construction of the Settle–Carlisle Railway, and the prehistoric peoples who inhabited the caves in the cliffs above the town.

On the western bank of the river from the old Settle Bridge, the Ribble Way continues up the valley following a contained path between school playing fields and the home ground of the town's football team, Settle United AFC. Briefly rejoining the river at the far end, dogleg through a squeeze stile from which a trod guides you across the centre of an open pasture. Climbing a wooded bank beyond, carry on along a path elevated above the river, shortly passing behind a farm. Over the next stile, opposite Langcliffe Mill, cut diagonally left, leaving the field across a stile beside a gate. To the right the lane takes you to Stackhouse, but over the stile opposite you can instead initially follow the field edge, rejoining the road a little further on when you meet the edge of a wood.

THE 'ANCIENT' WALL

Man farmed these slopes well before the Romans came to Britain, and on the hill behind Stackhouse is a curious stretch of drystone wall. About 70 yards (64m) long and about 5 feet (1.5m) high, it is better built than the nearby enclosure walls, and one theory suggests that it is over 2000 years old, although others are more sceptical and place it more realistically in the 18th century. ▶

Perhaps a settlement boundary or part of a stock enclosure, the wall's original purpose has now been lost in time, but it must have been of some importance as it represents a considerable investment in manual labour.

Just discernible on the OS map (grid ref SD802664), the wall lies a short distance from the Ribble Way. To see it, instead of returning to the lane from the field edge as you approach Stackhouse, follow the boundary of the wood above the houses where a signpost then directs you straight up the hill on a northwesterly course towards Feizor. After a little more than 1 mile (1.6km) you will see the wall over to the left of the path.

Keep with the main lane in the hamlet, but after 300 yards, immediately after a white cottage on the right, turn off onto a track. Signposted Locks, it takes you back to the Ribble where it is dammed by a weir, from which Langcliffe Mill drew its water. A path at the edge of successive fields continues upstream, later passing below a beech-wooded bank as the river turns behind Old Mill, which originally processed cotton, but was converted for the production of paper from rags in 1793. More recently it recycled waste paper into cardboard before closure in 2006. Keep going, once more gaining height above the water and then passing the outflow of Stainforth Beck. Skirting a camp site, Knight Stainforth Caravan and Camping Park, the river now runs in a small ravine and leads you on to Stainforth Force. ◀

At Stainforth Force the water cascades quite spectacularly over an abrupt limestone shelf, while in stark contrast the pool of water above it can lie as calm as a millpond.

The curious drystone wall above Stackhouse

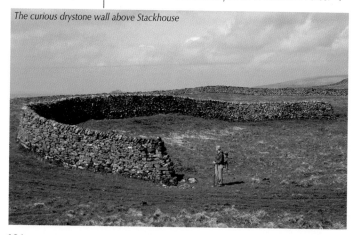

Leaving the riverbank at Stainforth Bridge, follow the lane over it, climbing to reach the main road. Go right and then left into Stainforth village.

Looking towards Langcliffe

STAINFORTH

Cared for by the National Trust, the graceful bridge of rough-hewn stones over the Ribble at Stainforth was built around 1670 and superseded a ford on an ancient packhorse route that ran between York and Lancaster. The village itself stands well above the Ribble, clustered around a stream of its own, Stainforth Beck. It has some charming secluded corners, such as the old stepping stones across the water above the bridge.

Nearby is the village inn, the Craven Heifer, one of several pubs hereabouts bearing the name. It celebrates a young cow bred in Gargrave at the beginning of the 19th century which weighed over a ton. The Craven Heifer achieved such local fame that the Craven Bank even used its image on a bank note issued in 1817.

With a pub and a choice of camp site or bunk house, you might be tempted to linger here for a while, and if you do, follow a walled track for a mile or so up the hill behind, where you will find Catrigg Force. This is one of the prettiest waterfalls in the Dales, the beck dropping abruptly in two steps through a narrow cleft of rock to a deep pool at the head of a wooded gorge, some 60 feet (18m) below.

At the bend beyond Stainforth's car park, go left and then keep ahead past a sign to Moor Head Lane, entering the hillside grazing pastures behind the village. Cross the first field to a stile, and over it bear right, striking upwards through old ploughing strips that terrace the valley. A grassy trod climbs determinedly onward over more stiles, eventually levelling onto the moorland enclosures above. As the unmistakable mass of Pen-y-ghent rises majestically in the middle distance, keep going for another ½ mile (800m) until you reach a lateral track, Moor Head Lane.

Stainforth Bridge

Climbing above How Beck towards Moor Head Lane

*The famous
Pen-y-ghent Café*

THE THREE PEAKS

The climb out of Stainforth offers a first glimpse of Whernside, just visible behind Park Fell to the north-west. Whernside rises to 2417 feet (736m) above sea level and is Yorkshire's highest peak. Ingleborough looms on the left across the valley, and at 2372 feet (724m) falls somewhat short of the optimistic 'mile high' suggested by Thomas Jefferys, the distinguished 18th-century geographer and map-maker. The third member of Yorkshire's Three Peaks, Pen-y-ghent, soars above the valley straight ahead of you, and although the most impressive-looking from here, it is actually the lowest of the group at a mere 2277 feet (694m).

The tradition of attempting to scale all of the three peaks in one day, known as 'the Three Peaks', began in 1887 when a couple of teachers from Giggleswick School, Canon J R Wynne-Edwards and D R Smith, extended further than intended what was supposed to be a day-out climb onto Ingleborough. They managed to also include both Whernside and Pen-y-ghent before darkness finally overtook them, and 10 years later the circuit had become a competition, with a record of under 10½ hours being set by four members of the Yorkshire Ramblers. Involving over 5000 feet (1525m) of ascent and nearly 24 miles (39km) of walking, the Three Peaks has since been done in less than four hours. But for mere mortals anything below 12 hours is no mean achievement, and you are then entitled to membership of the Three Peaks Club. Horton in Ribblesdale, the next village along the valley, has become established as the start and finish point for the Three Peaks, and you can register your attempt by punching in and out on a factory time clock at the Pen-y-ghent Café. However, if you do avail yourself of the service, make sure you remember to clock out at the end of the day, or ring in to explain your absence, otherwise the mountain rescue will be out looking for you!

It is a steep path up Pen-y-ghent from the south

If you want to take in Pen-y-ghent en route, continue forward across the moor to join the Pennine Way at Churn Mill Hole. It leads on ahead, the steep climb to the summit involving an easy scramble, before dropping off the western flank into Horton in Ribblesdale. The Ribble Way takes an altogether gentler route, but unfortunately relinquishes all the height recently gained as it follows Moor Head Lane left down to the road.

HORTON AND HELWITH BRIDGE QUARRIES

Moor Head Lane, the track down to Helwith Bridge, is part of an ancient monastic trackway that connected some of the disparate granges and estates of Fountains Abbey. Its course can be traced all the way from Kilnsey in Wharfedale right through to the great abbey's western-most lands at Borrowdale in the Lake District. As you follow the track into the valley your eye is inevitably drawn to the extensive quarries ranging across the opposite side, a succession of massive, raw scars that extend all the way up to Horton. Surprisingly, given that Helwith Bridge and Horton are so close together, the stone extracted at each is very different. Horton's industry is based on limestone, but at Helwith Bridge the uplift that created the Craven Fault brought to the surface the bedrock upon which the limestone was deposited. From the much older Silurian era, it rises in near-vertical slabs, and being hard and impervious to water it had a variety of uses, including paving, tombstones and the construction of water tanks. ◀

Some of the stone taken from Maughton Quarry found a ready market in Sheffield as whetstone for sharpening knife blades.

Walk left down the road to a junction and take the lane off towards Austwick, which leads over the railway and the Ribble, to the Helwith Bridge pub. Over a stile at the rear of the pub car park, cross the paddock behind and then bear left to emerge on a narrow lane. Opposite, a contained path parallels the lane to the right. At its end, re-cross to a gated track that passes beneath the

Horton in Ribblesdale and Pen-y-ghent

railway to the river. Ignoring the bridge across, head upstream, but as the river then swings away, slip over a waymarked stile and footbridge on the left to continue at the field edge beside the ongoing track. Over a ladder stile, keep ahead beyond the track's end to the far side of the next field.

Regaining the river, follow a track left to Craghill Farm. Continue through a couple of gates and carry on at the edge of successive fields, later passing through a delightful copse carpeted with flowers in spring. Beyond, a narrowing field ushers you to a footbridge on the right that spans a milky stream whose waters are heavy with lime from the quarries above. Carry on along the riverbank for a further ½ mile (800m), the path ultimately emerging onto a lane at the edge of Horton in Ribblesdale.

To go into the village take the footbridge to the car park and then turn right along the road. Otherwise follow the lane over the stone bridge, keeping ahead at the junction just beyond to reach the Crown Inn.

HORTON IN RIBBLESDALE

Standing at the southern end of Horton in Ribblesdale, and leaning gently to one side, Saint Oswald's Church certainly looks old, and indeed it is, claiming the only surviving Norman nave in the area. The doorway is from the same period and there is a fragment of early glass window, too, showing the head of Saint Thomas à Becket, murdered by four knights in Canterbury Cathedral on the veiled instructions of Henry II. The king later regretted his impetuosity and did public penance in an effort to assuage his guilt.

St Oswald's serves the whole of upper Ribblesdale, a community of farms and cottages scattered across the fellsides. ◀ The village itself grew on the back of the railway, the line having arrived in the 1870s. The limestone, which had previously been dug only to satisfy local needs, could now be economically

The typical 'yeoman' houses of the area reflected the growing general prosperity in English agriculture during the 18th century. This followed the enclosures Acts of 1750–1830, when independent farmers now owning their own land began to benefit from their investment in land and stock improvement.

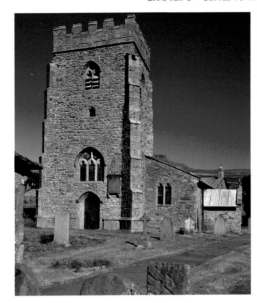

St Oswald's Church in Horton in Ribblesdale

taken out of the valley in great quantity, and the massive industrial quarries that are still worked were thus begun. Many of the houses in the village date from this period, built to accommodate the influx of workers and their families.

DAY WALKERS

Horton in Ribblesdale is the next stop north of Settle on the famous Settle–Carlisle railway line, along which a number of trains run morning and afternoon in each direction, offering a useful link between the start and end points of this section of the route. Alternatively, a fine circular walk can be devised taking in the summit of Pen-y-ghent. If you walk only as far as Stainforth or Helwith Bridge, there are also several less demanding valley-side return routes to choose from.

CHAPTER 7

Horton in Ribblesdale to
the Ribble's source

Distance	10.75 miles (17.3km) with a further 6 miles (9.7km) back to Ribblehead railway station
Height gain	1920 feet (585m)
Route assessment	After skirting the higher grazing of the valley, the landscape is of wild upland moors, the undulating way steadily rising and sometimes waterlogged away from established tracks
Time	5¾ hours to the source with a further 2½ hours back to Ribblehead
Public transport	Rail service between Horton in Ribblesdale and Ribblehead
Parking	Car park in Horton in Ribblesdale (pay-and-display) and by the road junction at Ribblehead
Refreshments	Café and choice of pubs at Horton in Ribblesdale; the Station Inn at Ribblehead
Toilets	Beside car park in Horton in Ribblesdale
Map	OS Explorer OL2, Yorkshire Dales (Southern & Western areas)

During the medieval period much of remote upper Ribblesdale was split between the monastic houses of Fountains, Furness and Sawley, who between them managed the land as extensive sheep walks for the production of wool. Apart from quarrying, this is still the main activity today, the sheep wandering far and wide across the lumpy hills. At one time there was also some mining for lead ore and coal, and on Fountains Fell behind Horton there is a 19th-century coke oven, used to produce fuel for roasting calamine (an ore of zinc) and lead ore. At the head of the valley is a vast, undulating moorland wilderness, distantly bounded by Whernside, Crag of Blea Moor and Cam Fell. Here the river changes both course and identity, abruptly turning onto the moor and, above Gearstones, assuming the name

Gayle Beck. Countless springs tumble down the slopes, each adding its sparkling contribution to the flow that will become the Ribble. Left to your own devices, you might be hard pressed to decide which is the most eligible candidate for the actual source, and indeed there is no consistency among earlier writers. Streams falling from the slopes of both Wold Fell and Cam Fell have been honoured in the past, but Gladys Sellers, who pioneered the route of the upper section of the Ribble Way, after careful consideration settled on a spring emanating below a low limestone scar at the head of Jam Syke on Gayle Moor. Her criteria: it is slightly higher than the other contenders; it describes the greatest distance to the sea; it flows throughout the year; and – perhaps most importantly from a walker's point of view – it is accessible by Right of Way. It is therefore to this spring above Jam Syke that this last leg of the walk takes you.

Walk past the front of the Crown Inn then swing left to follow a walled track that rises steadily along the valley side, taking the Ribble and Pennine Ways north from the village. A splendid view opens up as your height gradually increases, with the massive combined bulk of Ingleborough, Simon Fell and Park Fell grabbing your attention to the left. After 1 mile (1.6km) the way levels to twist across a dry gill, the water being snatched from its overland course by Sell Gill Pot, which lies just a few yards up the hill on the right.

The track up to Sell Gill Pot

In the past people steered well clear of these sinister chasms, as local legends claimed that they were the lairs of boggarts or evil goblins, who lured unwary travellers from the path and imprisoned them forever in the dark underworld.

SELL GILL POT

At the highpoint of the climb out of Horton, where the Pennine and Ribble Ways part company, you will find Sell Gill Pot, one of the many abrupt and gaping holes penetrating to the hidden world deep below this Swiss-cheese landscape. It swallows Sell Gill Beck, dropping 210 feet (64m) below the surface, and when first explored in 1897 was found to lead to a massive underground chamber, Yorkshire's second-largest known cavern. ◄

Through a gate just beyond the dry gill, abandon the main track as it swings to the right and walk forward to

Sell Gill Pot

a stile by an isolated laithe, or field barn. Circling the barn, carry on beside the right-hand wall, maintaining your direction as you pass from field to field below a low limestone escarpment. Ignore a path that forks off left after 1 mile (1.6km) and you will eventually reach an abrupt gully that cuts across your path. It can either be tackled directly, or by an easier line that winds around the head of the cleft to the right. Resuming your onward journey, bear gradually away from the left-hand wall, taking a higher course along the scar. After ¼ mile (400m) skirt the fenced head of a wooded gorge that falls steeply to High Birkwith, and joining a track, follow it left to pass through a gate.

Map continues p.118

BIRKWITH CAVE

At the end of the wall to the left is a stile giving access to the head of the ravine that you have just passed. Wander around to the left through the trees to find the entrance to Birkwith Cave, a wide, yawning horizontal gash at the base of a low cliff. A jumble of fallen boulders litters the mouth, and although the entrance gapes promisingly, you cannot progress far inside as it rapidly closes to a meagre slit. A lusty stream, however, gushes out, immediately cascading through a short, natural funnel worn through the rock, then dropping spectacularly into a narrow chasm that disappears among the trees below.

It is possible to clamber down to the cave entrance, and even follow the stream through the narrow pipe, but the exploration is not advised, for although a guide rope has been fixed, the wet rocks can be very slippery.

117

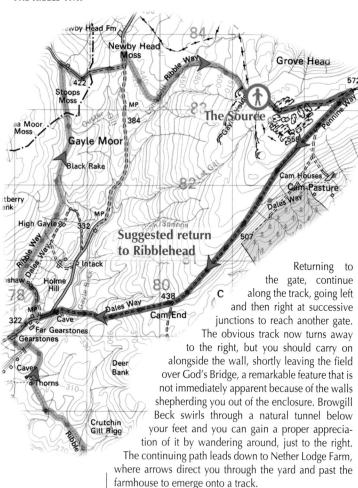

Returning to the gate, continue along the track, going left and then right at successive junctions to reach another gate. The obvious track now turns away to the right, but you should carry on alongside the wall, shortly leaving the field over God's Bridge, a remarkable feature that is not immediately apparent because of the walls shepherding you out of the enclosure. Browgill Beck swirls through a natural tunnel below your feet and you can gain a proper appreciation of it by wandering around, just to the right. The continuing path leads down to Nether Lodge Farm, where arrows direct you through the yard and past the farmhouse to emerge onto a track.

Instead of following it away to the left, cross to a faint trod opposite that strikes out onto the boggy moor, snaking through an undulating, untamed terrain of tussocky drumlins. Maintain your course for about 600 yards to find a stile in a fence – this is about 100 yards left of a more obvious gate – and beyond it the path becomes more distinct and soon leads to a stile and gate in a crossing wall.

NATURE RESERVE

Over to the right, on the hillside above Nether Lodge Farm, Cam Beck drops through a small gorge which, although not far below the tree line (around 1000 feet (305m) at this latitude) harbours a splendid mixed woodland of ash, hazel, hawthorn and willow. Like the grikes in limestone pavements, but on a very much larger scale, the surrounding cliffs provide shelter from the harsh prevailing elements and allow trees to assume their normal stature, while woodland spring flowers proliferate in the cover beneath. Although relatively small, the area is quite special and has national nature reserve protection.

Crumbling stone walls by the abandoned Thorns farmstead

Gayle Beck below Gearstones

The upper valley broadens to a landscape littered with small, vaguely egg-shaped hillocks called drumlins. Relics of the ice age, they were formed by slowly moving ice which created mounds in the underlying boulder clay, their 'pointed' ends showing the direction of the ice flow, which not unsurprisingly was down the length of the valley.

Keep going to reach the ruins of a barn, crossing another stile there before turning up past the building to a gate opening at the top of the hill. Now walk down to a derelict farmstead, Thorns, crossing a couple of walls to reach an enclosed track running between the buildings. Go right to a stile at its end and climb away to the left beside a wall. Keep ahead when it later recedes, cresting the hill to meet a crossing track. To the left, it leads to Gayle Beck, the headstream of the Ribble. After dry weather you can easily ford the flow, but when in flood it is best crossed by a bridge downstream. Through a gate on the opposite bank, bear slightly right to a stile and carry on up the next meadow to reach the road at Gearstones. ◀

LODGE HALL

On the opposite bank of the river, not far from where the road passes over the railway, there is a building now known as Lodge Hall. It is one of the area's finest surviving examples of a yeoman's house and was built by Christopher Weatherhead in 1687 – his initials are carved above the doorway together with the date. The farm had originally been a grange held by Furness Abbey, at the southwestern tip of Cumbria, and is just one more illustration of the vast extent of the medieval monastic estates.

THE SETTLE TO CARLISLE RAILWAY

This remote moor has witnessed man's regular passing for at least the last 2000 years. The most ambitious project was to bring through a railway from Settle to Carlisle, creating a link to Scotland for the Midland Railway Company and enabling it to compete with the already established routes following the east and west coasts. Work began in 1869 and took seven years to complete, forcing a 72 mile (116km) route across some of the wildest countryside in England. The track climbs to 1169 feet (356m) above sea level to cross the watershed into the Eden valley, and required the construction of 14 tunnels, 21 viaducts and a total of 325 bridges. The most spectacular section is here at Ribblehead, where a viaduct of 24 arches, the highest of which is 165 feet (50m), and two massive embankments carry the line for ¾ mile (1.2km) across the moor. The track then curves below the eastern flank of Whernside and disappears into the 1½ mile (2.4km) Blea Moor Tunnel to emerge at the head of Dentdale. The work was all undertaken by hand, and thousands of navvies were employed on the job, living with their families in rough camps that were periodically moved along as the work progressed. ▶

The line was one of the last main railway routes to be built in the country, and thrived for 100 years before suffering the decline experienced by much of the rest of the railway network from the late 1950s. By 1970 local services had ceased and closure looked inevitable, but tremendous popular support inspired a new service from Leeds, and later Preston, to Carlisle. The Dales Rail quickly proved so successful that by 1989 the line's future was secured.

Contemporary accounts describe the navvies' camps as something more appropriate to the Wild West than Victorian England.

The path onto Whernside

By any standards the completion of this railway line was a magnificent achievement, although the final cost highlights the considerable difficulties that were encountered. Construction took three years longer than had first been anticipated and the final bill came to nearly £3.5m, £1.3m more than the original estimate. The highest cost, however, was borne by the men who were employed to build it. It is said that 220 workers lost their lives in the all-too-frequent accidents that occurred during construction, one for every 3 miles (4.5km) of track. Countless more died, including wives and children, from smallpox and other diseases that ran rampant through the squalid settlements of hovels in which they lived. Some of the bodies were laid to rest in the churchyard of St Leonard's at nearby Chapel-le-Dale, where a plaque remembers their hardships. But their true and lasting memorial is surely here in this viaduct, an enduring monument to a pioneering vision and now the thrilling highlight of the country's most exciting railway journey.

Turn right along the B6255, passing Gearstones, which was once a cattle drovers' inn, and walk for a further ¼ mile (400m) before leaving the road along a track on the left opposite the entrance to Far Gearstones Farm. Marked as the Ribble Way and to Dent Head, it winds to a couple of houses. Keep ahead past them to climb straight up the hillside behind, staying with the wall on the right as it later turns to undulate easily along the valley. Maintain your forward line when the wall subsequently falls away below you, shortly joining a rising track, Black Rake Road.

Then, gently losing height, the track eventually ends at a lane, which you should follow right to its junction with the main road. Turn right, crossing to a gate from which a gravel track rises away across the flank of the hill. Later swinging around, it passes a rough hut to climb beside a deep clough. Before long, the path crosses Long Gill at a small cairn and then swings up beside Jam Syke. Higher up the trod crosses the stream, which subsequently, but briefly, asserts itself in a pronounced gully cleaving the shale beneath the boggy tussock. Above, the transition to limestone subtly alters the landscape; the path shortly re-crossing the stream to reach a gate. Abandon the track just before it and follow the diminishing stream to the foot of the low crag from which it issues, *la source*.

THE SOURCE

Before the introduction of modern mapping, it was no easy task to identify a single birthplace for the Ribble. While it is clear that it must lie somewhere within the great basin bounded by Crag of Blea Moor, Wold Fell and Cam Fell, there is a multitude of springs, rivulets and tiny streams to choose from. How you define your parameters also affects the choice: is it the furthest point from sea? the stream offering the most abundant flow? or that emanating from the highest point above sea level?, each in its way an equally valid criterion. ◄

Gladys Sellers considered the question when she extended the Ribble Way here in 1985, and determined that the springs on Gayle Wolds feeding Jam Syke were in fact the highest and, equally importantly, they trickled throughout the year. By chance, the spot is also accessible from a Right of Way and has become acknowledged as the true source of the Ribble.

After dry weather the beginning of the Ribble is little more than a dribble of crystal water seeping from the grey limestone rock of a low scar near the top of Cam Fell. Its early course is faltering and uncertain, and the trickle appears to be in imminent danger of being immediately swallowed up again by the earth from which it came. The rivulet's initial hesitant flow is marked not so much by a sliver of water, but by a ribbon of moss greened by the moisture. Quickly gathering the discharges of other

Not surprisingly, since the 19th century opinion among writers about the source of the Ribble has been divided, and several alternatives have been proclaimed in the past.

equally unpromising springs, lower down the stream soon becomes more obvious and gains a voice as it swells sufficiently to babble over the underlying stones. Despite the apparent bleakness of the location, it is not without life, for standing in silent guard over the insignificant puddle below the seep we found a small frog, and hiding beneath the stones of the pool were tiny freshwater shrimps. The wet rocks and crevices harbour mosses, lichen and small ferns, while spring brings a show of delicate flowers to brighten the thin grass.

An old stone barn near Sell Gill

On a fine day the view is splendid. Three valleys fall from the pass 400 feet (122m) below you. To the west the road drops into Dentdale, while to the right it descends along Widdale to Hawes, and further round and closer to hand is the head of Snazeholm Beck Dale, which runs into Widdale. To the left, of course, is Ribblehead, the massive viaduct striding confidently across the valley clearly evident in the middle distance. And if the wind is in the right direction you can even hear the distant rumble of the trains trundling slowly on their way. The backdrop is of two of Yorkshire's high peaks, Whernside

Journey's end, the source of the River Ribble

and Ingleborough, with Pen-y-ghent hidden from view by the hillside on which you stand. This is a spot to rest, enjoy the scenery and reflect upon your journey, perhaps enjoying a wee celebratory dram softened with pure water drawn from the source. From Longton you have walked at least 70 miles (113km), with the distance to and from refreshment, accommodation and exploring along the way to be added on top.

You are now 1840 feet (562m) above sea level, while without the sea wall the Dolphin Inn at the start of the route would be regularly flooded by incoming tides. However, the undulations of the path mean that you have climbed far more than that, around 6500 feet (1981m), and that is without bagging any of the tempting hills passed along the way. The path has taken you across the Ribble and its diminishing prime tributary a total of 11 times. How long have you taken to complete the Ribble Way? Well, that is a matter of personal choice and circumstance. While my colleague from the Long Distance Walker's Association tells me that some of the organisation's members might complete the full route in a 24-hour period, most people are content to adopt a more leisurely pace, leaving time to enjoy the scenery and investigate some of the places of interest passed during the journey.

All good things come to an end, however, and eventually you must get back onto your feet and return at least to Ribblehead for the night. You can of course retrace your steps down the hillside to the road and follow that, but an alternative route takes the old Roman road and turnpike over the moorland fell behind you. Go down the slope by the wall paralleling the stream to a block stile. Through it, turn sharp right and cut a diagonal line back up the hill past the corner of another wall to reach an expanse of grass-grown limestone pavement. As the gradient levels, bear left, eventually joining the line of a wall running from the right. Follow it on across a couple of disintegrating walls until you reach the corner where a gate lets you out onto a tarmac track, Cam High Road, at Cold Keld Gate.

CAM HIGH ROAD

The first road into the head of the Ribble valley was brought by the Romans. Crossing Cam Fell and carrying on along the Doe valley, it was part of a route linking the fort at Bainbridge with Lancaster. Cam High Road continued in use as a track throughout medieval times and was revived as a main thoroughfare in 1751 when the turnpike between Richmond and Lancaster adopted the same course. However, winter weather proved too much of a hazard on this lonely road over the tops, and by 1795 the way was diverted around Hawes and up Widdale, the line still followed by the present-day road, the B6255.

Through a gate to the right the track leads past the entrance to Cam Farm before striking a gentle and almost dead-straight descent along the hillside. After some 2¼ miles (3.6km), fork right at Cam End to remain on the Dales Way, the track dropping from the shoulder to a bridge across Gayle Beck. Climb to the road and follow it left for 1½ miles (2.4km) back to Ribblehead where you will find a pub offering food and accommodation, as well as the railway to take you home.

DAY WALKERS

The simplest option for drivers is to leave the car at Ribblehead and take a morning train to Horton in Ribblesdale. An inviting alternative that takes you onto the surrounding hills is to split the leg into two stages. The first would go from Horton to either Nether Lodge or Gearstones and return over Park Fell and the summit of Ingleborough. The final stage to the source is then the circular walk from Gearstones described in this chapter. However, please note that there is no official parking at Gearstones, and the National Park is anxious to avoid damage to the roadside verges. If coming by car, you are therefore asked to leave it at the designated parking by the junction at Ribblehead.

APPENDIX 1

Route Summary

Route Name	Distance	Height Gain	Time
Longton to Penwortham Bridge	7.5 miles (12.1km)	125 ft (38m)	3 hrs
Penwortham Bridge to Ribchester	11.9 miles (19.2km)	830 ft (253m)	5¼ hrs
Ribchester to Brungerley Bridge	11.5 miles (18.5km)	874 ft (266m)	5¼ hrs
Brungerley Bridge to Gisburn Bridge	9.3 miles (15km)	880 ft (268m)	4½ hrs
Gisburn Bridge to Settle	12.0 miles (19.3km)	780 ft (238m)	5½ hrs
Settle to Horton in Ribblesdale	7.5 miles (12km)	980 ft (299m)	3¾ hrs
Horton in Ribblesdale to the source	10.75 miles (17.3km)[a]	1920 ft (585m)	5¾ hrs[b]

[a] plus 6 miles (9.7km) back to Ribblehead railway station
[b] plus 2½ hrs back to Ribblehead

APPENDIX 2
Useful Information

Maps required:
OS Explorer 286, Blackpool & Preston
OS Explorer 287, West Pennine Moors
OS Explorer OL41, Forest of Bowland and Ribblesdale
OS Explorer OL2, Yorkshire Dales (Southern & Western areas)

Tourist Information
Lancashire and Blackpool Tourist Board, ☎ 01257 226600,
www.lancashiretourism.com

Preston Tourist Information Centre, Guild Hall, Lancaster Road, Preston
PR1 1HT, ☎ 01772 253731, email tourism@preston.gov.uk,
www.visitpreston.com

Clitheroe Tourist Information Centre, Ribble Borough Council Offices, Church
Walk, Clitheroe BB7 2RA ☎ 01200 425566

Yorkshire Dales and Harrogate Tourism Partnership, ☎ 01845 523877
www.yorkshiredalesandharrogate.com

Settle Tourist Information Centre, Town Hall, Cheapside, Settle BD24 9EJ,
☎ 01729 825192, email settle@ytbtic.co.uk

Horton in Ribblesdale Tourist Information Centre, Pen-y-ghent Café, Horton in
Ribblesdale, Settle BD24 0HE, ☎ 01729 860333, email horton@ytbtic.co.uk

Footpath Queries
Lancashire County Council, ☎ 01772 534709
North Yorkshire County Council Area Team, ☎ 0845 872 7374
Yorkshire Dales National Park, ☎ 0870 166 6333

Public Transport
Traveline, ☎ 0870 608 2 608

Main Access Points Served by Public Transport

Longton	Bus
Preston	Bus and rail
Ribchester	Bus
Hurst Green	Bus
Clitheroe	Bus and rail
Sawley	Bus
Gisburn	Bus
Rathmell	Bus
Settle	Bus and rail
Horton in Ribblesdale	Rail and infrequent bus
Ribblehead	Rail and infrequent bus

Early lambs near Winckley Hall

Clitheroe Castle

APPENDIX 3
Accommodation Listing

This accommodation list is not comprehensive and neither does it imply any recommendation of quality and standard – it is merely provided to help in planning an itinerary. Further information is available from local tourist information offices.

Longton
Willow Cottage, Thropps Lane West, off Longton Bypass, Longton, Preston PR4 5SW, ☎ 01772 617570, email willow.cottage@btconnect.com, **www.lancashirebedandbreakfast.com**. Bed and breakfast, luggage transport, evening meals available at nearby pubs and restaurant.

Preston
Ashwood Hotel, 11–13 Fishergate Hill, Preston, Lancashire PR1 8JB, ☎ 01772 203302, email enquiry@ashwoodhotel.co.uk, **www.ashwoodhotel.co.uk**. Bed and breakfast, evening meals available at nearby pubs and restaurants.
Jenkinson Farmhouse, Alston Lane, Longridge, Preston PR3 3BN, ☎ 01772 782624. Bed and breakfast, evening meals available at nearby pub and restaurant.

Hurst Green
Bayley Arms, Avenue Road, Hurst Green, Clitheroe BB7 9QB, ☎ 01254 826478, email sales@bayleyarms.co.uk, **www.bayleyarms.co.uk**
Pub accommodation serving meals.
Shireburn Arms Hotel, Whalley Road, Hurst Green, Clitheroe BB7 9QJ, ☎ 01254 826518, email sales@shireburnarmshotel.com, **www.shireburnarmshotel.com**.
Pub accommodation serving meals all day.
The Fold, 15 Smithy Row, Hurst Green, Clitheroe BB7 9QA, ☎ 01254 826252, email derek.harwood1@virgin.net. Bed and breakfast, meals available at nearby pub.

Ribchester
White Bull, Church Street, Ribchester PR3 3XP, ☎ 01254 ~~878303~~, email keithnewby@alice.it, ~~www.white-bull.co.uk~~.
Pub accommodation serving meals all day.

820 621
Food till 9pm

www.thewhitebullribchester.co.uk
Dble £85/night

Monday Quiz

Mitton
Aspinall Arms Hotel, Mitton Rd, Mitton, Clitheroe, Lancashire BB7 9PQ,
☎ 01254 826223, email simon@aspinallarms.co.uk, **www.aspinallarms.co.uk**.
Pub accommodation serving lunch and evening meals.

Clitheroe
The Camping & Caravanning Club Site, Edisford Road, Clitheroe BB7 3LA,
☎ 01200 425294. Camp site, meals available at nearby pub.
Brooklyn Guest House, 32 Pimlico Road, Clitheroe BB7 2AH,
☎ 01200 428268, mob 07974 307473, **www.brooklynguesthouse.co.uk**.
Bed and breakfast, evening meals available at nearby pub.
The Old Post House Hotel, 44–48 King Street, Clitheroe BB7 2EU,
☎ 01200 422025, email rooms@posthousehotel.co.uk, **www.posthousehotel.co.uk**.
Hotel accommodation serving lunch and evening meals.

Bolton-by-Bowland
The Coach and Horses (2 miles), 20 Main Street, Bolton-by-Bowland, Clitheroe
BB7 4NW, ☎ 01200 447202, email ross.heywood@btinternet.com,
www.boutiquedininghouse.co.uk. Pub accommodation serving lunch and
evening meals.

Gisburn
The White Bull, Main Street, Gisburn BB7 4HE, ☎ 01200 445575,
email whitebullhotel@aol.com, **www.thewhitebullhotel.co.uk**.
Pub accommodation serving meals all day.
Foxhill Barn, Howgill Lane, Gisburn BB7 4JL, ☎ 01200 415906,
email peter@foxhillbarn.co.uk, **www.foxhillbarn.co.uk**. Bed and breakfast, evening
meals and packed lunches by arrangement, luggage pickup and drop off.

Long Preston
Maypole Inn, Long Preston BD23 4PH, ☎ 01729 840219,
email robert@maypole.co.uk, **www.maypole.co.uk**. Pub accommodation serving
meals from lunch time onwards.

Wigglesworth
Cowper Cottage, Wigglesworth BD23 4RP, ☎ 01729 840598, email
marion.howard@btopenworld.com, **www.yorkshirenet.co.uk\stayat\cowper**.
Bed and breakfast, evening meals available at nearby inn.

Rathmell
Layhead Farm Cottages, Field House, Rathmell, Settle BD24 0LA,
☎ 01729 840234, email rosehyslop@layhead.co.uk, **www.layhead.co.uk**.
Bed and breakfast and self-catering accommodation.

Settle and Giggleswick
Pengarth, Austwick, North Yorkshire LA2 8BD, ☎ 01524 251073, email
jishreid@austwick.org. Bed and breakfast, evening meals available at nearby pub.
The Golden Lion Hotel, Duke Street, Settle BD24 9DU, ☎ 01729 822203,
email bookings@goldenlion.yorks.net, **www.goldenlionhotel.net**.
Pub/hotel accommodation serving meals.
The Harts Head Hotel, Belle Hill, Giggleswick, Settle BD24 0BA,
☎ 01729 822086, email info@hartsheadinn.co.uk, **www.hartsheadinn.co.uk**.
Pub/hotel accommodation serving evening meals.
The Oast Guest House, 5 Pen-y-Ghent View, Settle, BD24 9JJ,
☎ 01729 822989, email stay@oastguesthouse.co.uk, **www.oastguesthouse.co.uk**.
Bed and breakfast.
Mainsfield Guest House, Stackhouse Lane, Giggleswick, Settle BD24 0DL,
☎ 01729 823549, email mainsfield_bb@btopenworld.com,
www.mainsfieldguesthouse.co.uk. Bed and breakfast, evening meals available at
nearby pubs.

Stainforth
Knight Stainforth Caravan & Camping Park, Little Stainforth, Settle BD24 0DP,
☎ 01729 822200, email info@knightstainforth.co.uk,
www.knightstainforth.co.uk. Camp site, meals available at nearby pub.
Husband's Barn, Stainforth, Settle BD24 9PB, ☎ 01729 822240.
Bunk barn accommodation, evening meals available at nearby pub.
Craven Heifer, Stainforth, Settle BD24 9PB, ☎ 01729 822599,
email info@cravenheiferhotel.co.uk, **www.cravenheiferhotel.co.uk**.
Pub accommodation serving meals.

Helwith Bridge
The Helwith Bridge, Helwith Bridge, Settle BD24 0EH, ☎ 01729 860220.
Camping field beside pub that serves evening meals.

Horton in Ribblesdale
Crown Hotel, Horton in Ribblesdale BD24 0HF, ☎ 01729 860209,
email minehost@crown-hotel.co.uk, **www.crown-hotel.co.uk**.
Pub accommodation serving evening meals.

View above Stainforth

Golden Lion Hotel, Horton in Ribblesdale BD24 0HB, ☎ 01729 860206, email tricia@goldenlionhotel.co.uk, **www.goldenlionhotel.co.uk**. Hotel accommodation serving meals.
Broad Croft House, Horton in Ribblesdale BD24 0EX; ☎ 01729 860302; email cynthia@broadcroft.co.uk; **www.broadcroft.co.uk**. Bed and breakfast, packed lunches by arrangement
The Willows, Horton in Ribblesdale, Settle BD24 0HT, ☎ 01729 860200, mob 07800 765504, email johanne2@sky.com, **www.the-willows-horton-in-ribblesdale.co.uk**. Bed and breakfast, packed lunches, pick up and drop off, evening meals available at nearby pub.
Holm Farm Camp Site, Horton in Ribblesdale, Settle BD24 0HB, ☎ 01729 860281. Farm camp site open all year, evening meals available at nearby pubs.
3 Peaks Bunkroom, 1 Chapel Lane, Horton in Ribblesdale BD24 0HA; ☎ 01729 860380; email bookings@3peaksbunkroom.co.uk; **www.3peaksbunkroom.co.uk**, bunkhouse accommodation for groups of five or more, evening meals, breakfast and packed lunches from nearby pub.

Ribblehead
The Station Inn, Ribblehead, near Ingleton LA6 3AS, ☎ 01524 241274, email info@thestationinn.net, **www.thestationinn.net**. Pub and bunkhouse accommodation serving lunch and evening meals.

NOTES

NOTES

THE GREAT OUTDOORS
tgo

The UK's leading monthly magazine for the independent hilllwalker and backpacker. With thought provoking articles, varied and exhilarating routes, expert gear reviews and outstanding photography, TGO's writers are at the heart of the walking world providing the essentials to inspire your next adventure.

To subscribe today call

0141 302 7718

or visit **www.tgomagazine.co.uk**

Get ready for
take off

Adventure Travel helps you to go outdoors over there

More ideas, information, advice and entertaining features on overseas trekking, walking and backpacking than any other magazine – guaranteed.

Available from good newsagents or by subscription – 6 issues £15

Adventure Travel Magazine T:01789 488166

LISTING OF CICERONE GUIDES

ALPS – CROSS BORDER ROUTES
100 Hut Walks in the Alps
Across the Eastern Alps: E5
Alpine Points of View
Alpine Ski Mountaineering
  Vol 1: Western Alps
  Vol 2: Central and Eastern Alps
Chamonix to Zermatt
Snowshoeing
Tour of Mont Blanc
Tour of Monte Rosa
Tour of the Matterhorn
Walking in the Alps
Walks and Treks in the Maritime Alps
FRANCE
Écrins National Park
GR20: Corsica
Mont Blanc Walks
The Cathar Way
The GR5 Trail
The Robert Louis Stevenson Trail
Tour of the Oisans: The GR54
Tour of the Queyras
Tour of the Vanoise
Trekking in the Vosges and Jura
Vanoise Ski Touring
Walking in Provence
Walking in the Cathar Region
Walking in the Cevennes
Walking in the Dordogne
Walking in the Haute Savoie
  North
  South
Walking in the Languedoc
Walking in the Tarentaise &
  Beaufortain Alps
Walking on Corsica
Walking the French Gorges
Walks in Volcano Country
PYRENEES AND FRANCE/SPAIN
CROSS-BORDER ROUTES
Rock Climbs In The Pyrenees
The GR10 Trail
The Mountains of Andorra
The Pyrenean Haute Route
The Way of St James
  France
  Spain
Through the Spanish Pyrenees: GR11
Walks and Climbs in the Pyrenees
SPAIN & PORTUGAL
Costa Blanca Walks
  Vol 1: West
  Vol 2: East
The Mountains of Central Spain
Trekking through Mallorca
Via de la Plata
Walking in Madeira
Walking in Mallorca
Walking in the Algarve
Walking in the Canary Islands:
  Vol 2: East
Walking in the Cordillera Cantabrica
Walking in the Sierra Nevada
Walking the GR7 in Andalucia
Walks and Climbs in the Picos de
  Europa

SWITZERLAND
Alpine Pass Route
Central Switzerland
The Bernese Alps
Tour of the Jungfrau Region
Walking in the Valais
Walking in Ticino
Walks in the Engadine
GERMANY
Germany's Romantic Road
King Ludwig Way
Walking in the Bavarian Alps
Walking in the Harz Mountains
Walking in the Salzkammergut
Walking the River Rhine Trail
EASTERN EUROPE
The High Tatras
The Mountains of Romania
Walking in Bulgaria's National Parks
Walking in Hungary
SCANDINAVIA
Walking in Norway
SLOVENIA, CROATIA AND
MONTENEGRO
The Julian Alps of Slovenia
The Mountains of Montenegro
Trekking in Slovenia
Walking in Croatia
ITALY
Central Apennines of Italy
Gran Paradiso
Italian Rock
Italy's Sibillini National Park
Shorter Walks in the Dolomites
Through the Italian Alps
Trekking in the Apennines
Treks in the Dolomites
Via Ferratas of the Italian Dolomites:
  Vols 1 & 2
Walking in Sicily
Walking in the Central Italian Alps
Walking in the Dolomites
Walking in Tuscany
Walking on the Amalfi Coast
MEDITERRANEAN
Jordan – Walks, Treks, Caves, Climbs
  and Canyons
The Ala Dag
The High Mountains of Crete
The Mountains of Greece
Treks & Climbs in Wadi Rum, Jordan
Walking in Malta
Western Crete
HIMALAYA
Annapurna: A Trekker's Guide
Bhutan
Everest: A Trekker's Guide
Garhwal & Kumaon: A Trekker's and
  Visitor's Guide
Kangchenjunga: A Trekker's Guide
Langtang with Gosainkund &
  Helambu: A Trekker's Guide
Manaslu: A Trekker's Guide
The Mount Kailash Trek

NORTH AMERICA
British Columbia
The Grand Canyon
The John Muir Trail
SOUTH AMERICA
Aconcagua and the Southern Andes
AFRICA
Climbing in the Moroccan Anti-Atlas
Kilimanjaro: A Complete Trekker's
  Guide
Trekking in the Atlas Mountains
Walking in the Drakensberg
IRELAND
Irish Coastal Walks
The Irish Coast to Coast Walk
The Mountains of Ireland
EUROPEAN CYCLING
Cycle Touring in France
Cycle Touring in Ireland
Cycle Touring in Spain
Cycle Touring in Switzerland
Cycling in the French Alps
Cycling the Canal du Midi
Cycling the River Loire
The Danube Cycleway
The Grand Traverse of the Massif
  Central
The Way of St James
INTERNATIONAL CHALLENGES,
COLLECTIONS AND ACTIVITIES
Canyoning
Europe's High Points
AUSTRIA
Klettersteig – Scrambles in the
  Northern Limestone Alps
Trekking in Austria's Hohe Tauern
Trekking in the Stubai Alps
Trekking in the Zillertal Alps
Walking in Austria
TECHNIQUES
Indoor Climbing
Map and Compass
Mountain Weather
Moveable Feasts
Outdoor Photography
Rock Climbing
Snow and Ice Techniques
Sport Climbing
The Book of the Bivvy
The Hillwalker's Guide to
  Mountaineering
The Hillwalker's Manual
MINI GUIDES
Avalanche!
Navigating with a GPS
Navigation
Pocket First Aid and Wilderness
  Medicine
Snow

For full and up-to-date information
on our ever-expanding list of guides,
please visit our website:
www.cicerone.co.uk.

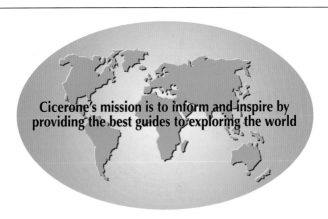

Cicerone's mission is to inform and inspire by providing the best guides to exploring the world

Since its foundation 40 years ago, Cicerone has specialised in publishing guidebooks and has built a reputation for quality and reliability. It now publishes nearly 300 guides to the major destinations for outdoor enthusiasts, including Europe, UK and the rest of the world.

Written by leading and committed specialists, Cicerone guides are recognised as the most authoritative. They are full of information, maps and illustrations so that the user can plan and complete a successful and safe trip or expedition – be it a long face climb, a walk over Lakeland fells, an alpine cycling tour, a Himalayan trek or a ramble in the countryside.

With a thorough introduction to assist planning, clear diagrams, maps and colour photographs to illustrate the terrain and route, and accurate and detailed text, Cicerone guides are designed for ease of use and access to the information.

If the facts on the ground change, or there is any aspect of a guide that you think we can improve, we are always delighted to hear from you.

Cicerone Press
2 Police Square Milnthorpe Cumbria LA7 7PY
Tel: 015395 62069 Fax: 015395 63417
info@cicerone.co.uk www.cicerone.co.uk

CICERONE